Katharine Schuyler Baxter

In Bamboo Lands

Katharine Schuyler Baxter

In Bamboo Lands

ISBN/EAN: 9783337169770

Printed in Europe, USA, Canada, Australia, Japan

Cover: Foto ©Andreas Hilbeck / pixelio.de

More available books at **www.hansebooks.com**

IN BAMBOO LANDS

BY
KATHARINE SCHUYLER BAXTER

ILLUSTRATED

New York
THE MERRIAM COMPANY
67 Fifth Avenue

To the Public,

I dedicate the simple truth.

PREFACE.

The Empire of Japan has long been an object of interest to he Western world. A generous destiny enabled me to visitt those attractive islands and to gain an insight not only into the delightful customs of the great common people, but into the arts and the industries, and into the beautiful and touching worship of ancestors as well. In the following simple and impartial recital of what I saw and did in the course of a pleasurable tour, I have endeavored not to increase the bulk of the volume by extraneous digression or by my own reflections. Those who are interested in Japanese art will find brief descriptions of the manufacture of pottery, damascene, cloisonné, and lacquer. The illustrations are reproductions of pictures gathered during my travels. I desire to acknowledge my indebtedness to Dr. J. J. Rein, to the columns of *The Japan Mail*, and for invaluable assistance derived from the works of the distinguished author, Mr. B. H. Chamberlain, of Tōkyō. That this unpretentious chronicle may prove as enjoyable to the reader as did the journey through Dai Nippon to the tourist is the earnest wish of the

AUTHOR.

CONTENTS.

	PAGE
CHAPTER I.	
THE QUEEN'S HIGHWAY,	13
CHAPTER II.	
AROUND TŌKYŌ BAY,	36
CHAPTER III.	
NIKKŌ AND THE NORTH,	84
CHAPTER IV.	
TŌKYŌ,	139
CHAPTER V.	
THE TŌKAIDŌ,	205
CHAPTER VI.	
KYŌTŌ,	238
CHAPTER VII.	
MUTSUHITO AND HARUKO,	345
CHAPTER VIII.	
THE INLAND SEA,	360
GLOSSARY OF JAPANESE WORDS,	379

LIST OF ILLUSTRATIONS.

	PAGE
A Grove of Bamboo,	Frontispiece
The Valley of the Bow,	17
Lake Agnes, 8,000 feet above sea-level,	20
"Sir Donald" and the Great Glacier of the Selkirks,	23
The Loops,	24
Illicilliwaet River and Hermit Range, Selkirk Mountains,	25
Fraser River at Yale,	28
Yokohama Bay from "The Bluff,"	37
A Kuruma,	41
Blind Shampooer,	43
The One Hundred Steps,	44
Tea-House,	47
Pilgrims to Fujiyama,	51
A Dashi or Religious Car,	53
Mississippi Bay,	57
Daibutsu,	61
Enoshima,	65
Shrine of Yoritomo,	67
A Fan,	68
Motomachi,	69
The Grand Avenue,	73
The Bronze Bell,	77
A Daikon Vender,	79
The Torii and Pagoda,	81
Bronze Lanterns,	85
Holy Water Cistern,	89
Gifts to "Old Japan,"	93
Yomeimon Gate,	97
Gate of the Chapel of Ieyasu,	101
Moss-grown Steps to the Tomb of Ieyasu,	105

List of Illustrations.

	PAGE
Tomb of Ieyasu,	109
Yashamon Gate, Iemitsu,	113
Sacred Images of Amida,	117
Lake Chûzenji,	119
A Kago,	121
A Cascade,	125
Salutation,	127
Yumoto Lake,	129
Ainos of Yezo,	131
Japanese Junk,	132
Yumoto Springs,	133
A Japanese House Boat,	137
The Fire Department,	141
Shiba. Gateway No. 1,	145
Shiba,	147
Koto,	150
Koto,	150
Gekkin,	152
Samisen,	153
Interior of Japanese House,	154
Dwarf Trees,	155
Japanese Musicians,	160
Dancing Girls,	162
Official Harakiri,	165
Temple of Kameido,	168
Wistaria,	170
The Lotus Pond, Ueno Park,	172
Daibutsu, Ueno,	175
Residence of Count Ōkuma,	179
Street Decorations,	183
Game of Sai,	184
The Sumida River, near Tokyo,	185
Wrestling,	190
Botanic Gardens,	191
A Warrior in Full Uniform,	193
Daibutsu, Asakasa,	199
The Bell Temple at Asakasa,	202
On the Road to Miyanoshita,	207

List of Illustrations.

	PAGE
Dogashima, near Miyanoshita,	209
Fujiyama,	211
The Fishing Industry,	215
Rice Fields,	219
Sifting Rice,	223
Golden Dolphin,	227
Gifu in Ruins,	231
Temple of Chion-in,	241
Waking up the Gods,	243
The Great Bell,	247
Ancient Coin,	249
San-jū-san-gen-lō,	251
Nishi Otani,	256
Megane-bashi,	257
Kurodani,	259
A Wedding Ceremony,	263
Kiyomizu-dera,	267
Wash-Day,	270
Buddhist Priests,	273
Shintō Priest,	275
Tea-House,	279
Tea Harvest,	281
The Palace of the Mikado,	285
Street in Kyōtō,	289
Bamboo Ware for Sale,	291
Pine Tree at Karasaki,	295
A Shop,	303
A Family Dinner-Party,	307
Golden Pavilion, Kinkakuji,	309
A Pine-Tree Trained in the Form of a Junk,	313
A Farmer,	317
A Geisha,	322
A Hand-Loom,	326
Inari,	329
A Theatre,	331
The Old Castle and Moat at Ōsaka,	335
Tennōji, Ōsaka,	337
A Samurai,	345

List of Illustrations.

	PAGE
A View of Castle, and Nijiubashi,	347
The Palace,	349
The Emperor,	352
A Flower-Vender,	353
The Empress,	355
A Shintō Shrine, Kōbe,	357
The Inland Sea,	361
Miyajima, the Great Torii,	365
Nagasaki,	369
A Buddhist Temple,	372
On the Road to Moji,	373
Wrestlers,	376

IN BAMBOO LANDS.

CHAPTER I.

THE QUEEN'S HIGHWAY.

To travel widely abroad is an education in itself—it teaches a cosmopolitanism that one can never learn from books. To see ancient civilizations, other types of humanity, and other variations of scenery, is a source of such endless delight that when an urgent request came from friends to join them in Yokohama I made hurried preparations and started at once.

The train that bore me westward left the station at Montreal one sultry evening in August. I was fortunate at the outset in making the acquaintance of a gentleman and his wife who had started on their fourth tour of the world. They proved to be most agreeable fellow-travellers. As they had been careful not to have the stamps removed, their baggage was a curiosity, and nearly every place of importance on the globe was represented. The following day we travelled through a grim, dreary region. At one time in the geological history of America the land was covered with ice, and marks of the glacial period can still be observed on the rock-strewn soil. Pine trees sharply outlined against the sky towered above us, their naked

In Bamboo Lands.

trunks scarred by forest fires. The scant undergrowth added to the general desolation. The second morning the scenery had entirely changed. As our train approached Lake Superior, the dense forest was broken here and there, affording us glimpses of its rocky headlands and deep-blue waters.

We made a short stop at Port William, an old trading-post of the Hudson's Bay Company, now a depot of supplies and a shipping-point of the Canadian Pacific Railway. The abandoned boats used by Sir Garnet Wolseley, in his expedition against the Riel Rebellion in 1870, could still be seen while crossing Eagle River. They were fast falling to decay, and looked strangely out of place in that wild and rugged country. All through this region the streams abound in fish, and berries grew in abundance beside the way. It made our hearts ache with envy to view the rivers with no time to fish them, but at every little stopping-place the passengers rushed forth *en masse* to gather the luscious blackberries—merry scenes in which tourists, emigrants, and backwoodsmen mingled in picturesque groups.

We came upon the Lake of the Woods, a fine sheet of water of indescribable beauty and loneliness. Pine-covered islands dot the surface and wooded promontories jut far out into the dark water, and, except for a few wild-fowl, I did not see a sign of life.

Gradually we left the timber belt behind, as we neared Winnipeg and the fertile region of the Red River. Here a new country begins, and we were soon in the great wheat-fields of the Northwest. Winnipeg is now a thriving city of many

The Queen's Highway.

handsome buildings, and is lighted by electricity. We walked up the main street to the site of old Fort Garry, of which nothing remained to indicate the spot but the ruined gateway. The Hudson's Bay Company have in recent years removed their interests from the fort to a fine large store, where they conduct a flourishing business in every article but pelts.

Four hundred miles farther on begin the plains which, not so many years ago, were the feeding-grounds of vast herds of buffalo, now almost extinct. From the car windows, we observed the well-defined trails made in going to and from their watering-places. These prairies, which extend to the Rockies, are covered with an abundance of yellow-brown grass, and are unbroken, except by the lines of trees that mark the watercourses. They are strewn with buffalo horns, which the Indians collect, and the squaws polish, mount, and sell at all the prairie stations. The Sioux display great ingenuity in making up bright-colored blankets into fantastic costumes, in which the braves with natural vanity pose against a background of station buildings.

The Canadian Mounted Police in gay uniforms are noticeable figures all through the Northwest. Attired in red coats with gold buttons, high-topped boots, and absurd little caps held in place by straps, they are favorite subjects for the camera. Chasing Indians and bringing them to justice seem an occupation unworthy of so much elegance.

As our train penetrated the Rockies, that rise abruptly from the plain, the scenery steadily became grander until we reached Banff Station, in the Canadian National Park—a tract to be

In Bamboo Lands.

kept in its present wild and natural state for all time. A drive of three miles brought us to Banff village, amid some of the grandest scenery in America. The hotel, perched on an elevation at the junction of two lovely rivers, is surrounded on all sides by mountains from 8,000 to 11,000 feet high. From the veranda a magnificent panorama is disclosed of Tunnel Mountain, a frowning precipice with wooded base; the lofty crags that form the Twin Peaks; the Castle Mountain range, covered with perpetual snow; while below us, in the ravine thickly grown with maples and evergreens, the Bow River plunges seventy feet from the rocks to unite with the Spray. There are fine drives through the valley and around Tunnel Mountain and bridle-paths leading to Warm Sulphur Springs. Unfinished trails penetrate the wildest forest and to heights from which grand views may be obtained.

In pre-railroad days the Park was a mysterious, unexplored country, in which wild game roamed undisturbed. Its brooks and rivers are supplied with water-fowl and fish. Except at the highest points, it is nearly covered with a dense growth of trees of the evergreen group. Many of the trees are of great size, and stand so closely together that it is difficult for a man to pass between them. Where the trees are not so thick, the undergrowth seems determined to conquer everything.

I had read too many old-time adventures with Bruin to think of spending a week in the lonely Rockies without seeing a grizzly; so I consulted a guide, who assured me that wild animals did haunt the remoter ranges, but were "never seen in these parts." My fears were set at rest. For three days we

THE VALLEY OF THE BOW.

The Queen's Highway.

scaled many a steep hilltop, rambled through the forest, or followed the course of streams literally surrounded by nature. Many of these trails wander for a mile or more and then "run up a tree." Sometimes there was not a trace of a path. We saw many varieties of plumage and song birds, and occasionally an eagle would swoop down from the top of a pine and sail away across the valley out of sight. It was the silence of the forest, the untamed luxuriance of the out-of-doors, that I love.

The sunsets were magnificent, and one evening, while we were watching the stately ceremony from the piazza, a large black bear was seen trotting along the highway. In the excitement that ensued he escaped and with him fled all zest for exploration. The rest of the time we devoted to other pursuits. Whole days were spent on the Bow River and its tributaries, paddling in birch-bark canoes and fishing with rod and fly in the clear water, fanned by the faint breeze of the woods. We could see the fish calmly lying in the shadows of the rocks; and occasionally a whole school of trout would swim slowly around our flies, as if debating which should have the first bite. It was not exciting sport, as food is abundant, and the wary, well-fed creatures refused to be caught. Our experience was not unlike that of the hunter who, after an unsuccessful day, asked a woodman if there was "any hunting around here," and was answered, "Yes, you can hunt around here forever and get nothing."

Learning, while at Banff, that the steamer in which we were to sail for Japan would be detained for a period of two days, we decided to visit other points of interest.

In Bamboo Lands.

The train took us to Laggan, a station thirty miles to the west. Thence we made an upward climb of three miles by stage to the Lakes of the Clouds, of matchless coloring. They lie one above the other, high up, among gigantic peaks and fields of snow, reflecting in their crystal waters the forests, cliffs, and lofty summits of their prison walls. Birds had entirely disappeared at these altitudes, but lovely wild-flowers grew in sheltered spots along the trail. The air was cool and bracing, and the views were unsurpassed for beauty and grandeur. We could see far down the deep and narrow gorges, and magnificent mountain ranges rearing their lofty summits far above the misty realm of cloudland. It was amid such surroundings that we spent the night at a log chalet—a sweet, quiet place, picturesquely situated on the shore of Lake Louise, the lowest of that "trio of lakelets." The evening was not dull that our tired party spent in the comfortable sitting-room before a fire of unsawed cordwood, detailing our experiences in that country of crag and canyon.

Early in the morning, we rode down through the forest to the station and resumed our journey. Mount Stephen, 12,000 feet high, was seen from different points as we swept through the canyons walled in by Cyclopean peaks and dizzy precipices. Suddenly we left the Rockies and plunged into the Selkirks. We crawled around wooded mountain-sides, we crossed bridges three hundred feet above roaring torrents, and reached the Glacier House, at the foot of Mount Sir Donald, that same afternoon. Sir Donald and the glacier looked very beautiful in the bright sunshine and magnificent in the brilliant sunset.

LAKE AGNES, 8,000 FEET ABOVE SEA LEVEL.

The Queen's Highway.

We walked up the ravine two miles to the glacier and mounted its grimy cliffs, that lose much of their whiteness on close acquaintance. Grand as it is, it scarcely equals the Alpine and is much less impressive than the Alaskan. The mountains

"SIR DONALD" AND THE GREAT GLACIER OF THE SELKIRKS.

that wall in this valley and its glacier-fed stream lift their cloud-capped heights to an altitude of ten thousand feet.

That evening, under the guidance of an old miner, who had remarked, "I'll take ye's all," an excursion was planned for the following day. As the outing promised to be both instructive and amusing, the party numbered twenty-eight, and, provided with staves, we started down the valley to inspect that

In Bamboo Lands.

THE LOOPS.

railway wonder known as "The Loops." The track descends six hundred feet in two miles, crossing two ravines by a series of curves and loops to reach the deep valley below—a marvellous example of engineering skill. The day was delightful and

ILLICILLIWAET RIVER AND HERMIT RANGE. SELKIRK MOUNTAINS.

The Queen's Highway.

the mountain air delicious. We climbed the hillsides, crossed mountain streams, crawled over boulders, collected minerals, gathered berries and wild flowers, spread our lunch on a shelving rock, and drank from the sweet, cool brook that flowed beneath. Our guide was anxious we should see everything, and we did; and that is the reason why one over-fatigued individual declared we had tramped eighty miles instead of eight. I left Glacier with real regret.

On crossing the headwaters of the Columbia, I asked myself if this narrow stream were the same river I had seen hurling itself over the rocks at The Dalles, sweeping majestically past old Vancouver and dashing itself into the Pacific at Astoria. We passed through the Gold Range, less lofty but more beautifully wooded, down to the shore of Shuswap Lake, glistening in all the glory of sunset. The scenery was as magnificent as on the previous day.

The ride down the Fraser River canyon was the most exciting feature of the trip. Far to the west stretched the gorge, its walls, precipitous for the most part, rising grandly hundreds of feet high on either side. The railroad is cut out of the cliff, far above the roaring waters, and the train rushes down the dark ravine through tunnels and around curves for hours, until the mountains recede and the river broadens. Encampments of Indians engaged in catching and curing salmon, which they enclose in boxes and place high up in the branches of tall trees, out of reach of bears and other climbing animals, were located all through the Fraser valley. Bruin, one fancies, might be trusted quite as much as some members

In Bamboo Lands.

of their own fraternity. The grandeur and variety of scenery we had passed through from the moment we entered the Rockies is indescribable; and, seated in an observation car, we studied the ever-changing panorama. Stretched before us were canyons, wooded heights, mighty rivers, glaciers, and snow-covered spires rising upward until cloud and sky and peak com-

FRASER RIVER AT YALE.

mingled in one vast and bewildering vision. We had surfeit of the beautiful. "Furs, fins, and feathers" abound in that paradise of the adventurous sportsman. The scenery of the other transcontinental roads is inferior to this, since one can look upon a lofty mountain from summit to base without a foothill to intervene.

The Queen's Highway.

Our land journey ended at Vancouver—a young, ambitious city with a fine harbor, a beautiful park, and real estate agents enough to buy and sell every foot of land on the coast. It is less than a decade since the place was laid out on a magnificent scale; and already it has many fine commercial blocks of stone, and handsome residences with well-kept lawns brilliant with roses, which grow to perfection in that climate. Vast numbers of unbuilt squares, covered with stumps of the Douglas pine, disfigure the town; if these are ever built upon they will make Vancouver a mighty city. The shops are rather attractive, especially those in which Alaska Indian work and Oriental products are displayed. The city has wonderful advantages of splendid mountain and superb ocean views, far and near; besides many miles of drives through woods and along the seashore to Sea Island and Lulu Island. The most charming is the nine-mile drive through Stanley Park—a natural forest of giant Douglas pine, with thick undergrowth of smaller trees, shrubs, and ferns entangled with vines and creepers. Among the many beautiful parasites that run riot are the birds-nest ferns that grow in great profusion on the overhanging branches. We drove through the woods to a cliff where, on the rocks below, lay the wreck of the *Beaver*, the first steamer that ever ploughed the Pacific. It was sent around Cape Horn in 1836 by the Hudson's Bay Company, and did duty on the coast for half a century, until dashed on the rocks of Burrard Inlet.

An electric road through the forest connects Vancouver with New Westminster on the Fraser River; a flourishing place before the Canadian Pacific Railroad made Vancouver

In Bamboo Lands.

its terminus. Its chief industry is the canning of salmon, and shipping it to all parts of the world. The river swarms with boats, from which the Indians scoop the fish out of the water with big landing-nets, a piscatory device a degree higher than the wheel used on the Columbia.

The harbor filled with shipping, and its shores lined with warehouses, present a lively scene, particularly on sailing-day, when the townspeople throng the wharves to see the steamer off. We embarked on the *Empress of India* amid all the bustle attending departure on long voyages. Loud cheers came from a hundred throats as the big steamer swung loose and dropped slowly down the Narrows into the Gulf of Georgia, studded with innumerable islands. Snow-capped Mount Baker, towering to a height of 14,000 feet, was in sight for hours, and was the last we were to see of our native land until twelve long months had passed.

That evening we touched at Victoria, where, in addition to other passengers and freight, we took on board three hundred Chinamen (who go and come by every ship by the hundreds) and the dead bodies of sixty more. A Chinese loves the land of his birth with a superstitious reverence, and it is his lifelong wish to be buried there. If he is so unfortunate as to die in foreign parts, no matter how great the distance, he insures that his remains shall be taken to "the Flowery Kingdom" for final rest.

As land faded from sight we settled down to the enjoyment of the voyage. The ship was not crowded. We had large airy staterooms, every arrangement for delightful baths, luxurious

The Queen's Highway.

chairs on the broad promenade decks, and the food was excellent; every comfort was provided for, but we had reckoned without the weather, and that was execrable. The course taken by this line of steamers is a northerly one; and after the first day fogs, rains, and rousing winds had full sway, and for twenty-four hours very few persons were present at the table. Two days were spent in the seclusion of my cabin, for I know of no better remedy for seasickness than to go to my berth and remain there until it runs its horrid course. When partially recovered, I feebly sought the fresh air; but an icy wind blew across the wet and slippery decks, and the warmest wraps gave insufficient protection. My last resort was the library, where I sat day after day devouring all the books I could find on China and Japan, and deriving both pleasure and profit while the gale increased and the staunch ship tossed and tumbled in tempestuous seas. Sir Harry Parkes was England's most "trusty and able" representative in the "Far East for a period of forty-three years." He held various consular posts in China, and was taken prisoner during the war of 1860 and tortured. "In 1865 he was appointed Minister Plenipotentiary and Envoy Extraordinary to the Court of Yedo, which post he continued to hold until 1883." During the revolution of 1868, which resulted in the overthrow of the Shogun and the restoration of the Mikado to his ancient rights, Sir Harry, with great foresight, "threw the whole weight of British influence into the loyal side against the rebels." In 1883 he was promoted as British Minister to the Court of Peking, where he died in 1885. His career both in China and in Japan showed great strength

In Bamboo Lands.

of character, and his sunny smile and genial manner attracted to him all with whom he came into contact. My seat at table was next that of his eldest daughter, a charming lady and the wife of an English gentleman residing in Hong-Kong. Such was my good fortune, we became warm friends; but I did not learn of her distinguished parentage until I reached Yokohama. She remained with her children and her younger sister in Japan until late in autumn; I was her guest on several occasions, and she could not have been kinder. The letters of introduction I had taken were unnecessary; her influence gave me the *entrée* of all I wished to see and secured me a gracious reception.

The monotony of life on board was varied by a distant view of an outlying island of the Aleutian group, a flaring display of aurora borealis with splendors of color impossible to describe, and the reported deaths of three Celestials in the steerage. There were no burials at sea, however; their compatriots embalmed the remains, and I suppose they now rest in ancestral ground.

The Chinese stewards, dressed in white cotton garments, were a feature of the ship. Quiet, faithful, and attentive,— too attentive on occasion,—they have a habit of entering one's cabin without ceremony at most unseasonable times. One afternoon while enjoying a nap on my lounge, I was suddenly aroused by my steward, who said: "You wake up now. I see you sleep, dinner he ready." This incident occurred the day we crossed the 180th meridian, and the two combined made a lasting impression.

The Queen's Highway.

As we were entirely out of the track of commerce, not a ship was sighted until we neared the Japan coast.

Day after day we moved steadily on in the wintry air. The storm ceased as we entered the Japan Stream; the atmosphere was no longer cold, but full of moisture. Furs and heavy clothing were laid aside, and lighter garments were in requisition.

In traversing the vast expanse of the Pacific half a score of times, I have always found that misnamed ocean in a passionate, hateful mood, and it kept up its bad temper to the end. The last day we ran into an outer circle (I have no curiosity to make practical acquaintance with an inner section) of one of those revolving storms or typhoons that are so disastrous to shipping on that coast. According to schedule, we should have reached our destination, Yokohama, on a certain day; but the wind lashed the sea into foam, and the steamer was compelled to lie off the harbor all night. The storm obscured all objects of interest as we steamed up Tōkyō Bay, where we dropped anchor about two miles from land. To disembark was well-nigh impossible; the hurricane had left the sea still agitated, and the captain wisely decided to wait until the waves subsided before approaching the shore.

As there are no wharves in Yokohama, passengers are obliged to land in small boats. We were at once surrounded by a swarm of sampans—clumsy-looking native boats, heavily and strongly put together with wooden bolts. Flat-bottomed and flat-sided, the bow is high and pointed, the stern nearly square; they are sculled by two or more men standing up, and

In Bamboo Lands.

managed with great skill. I cannot in truth say that the boatmen were dressed, as they wore only a wide-sleeved scanty garment open at the neck and not reaching to the knees, and a strip of cloth knotted on the forehead. The material of the dress was cotton, cheap and coarse, and blue in color. This was full dress for the adults. The lads were nude except for the maro, or loin cloth, which the law compels them to adopt. Their limbs, bare and unshapely, were ornately tattooed. I noticed one whose yellow skin was well covered with some hideous creature; the opening in his one garment disclosed the head resting on his chest and the other extremity wound about his leg. While the natives waited excitedly for passengers and freight, they kept up a constant chatter, and in their eager haste they bumped and jostled each other with great good-nature, using the cry of "Hai!" "Hai!" as a precautionary signal. The sampans were so tightly packed that you could have walked over the solid, moving, changing floor of boats.

The officers discouraged all attempts at leaving the ship; but one passenger, a very stout lady, was determined to go at all hazards. She signalled a steam-launch and was assisted on board, while the small craft rose and sank frightfully in the rough sea. The boat rocked so terribly, it was impossible for her to enter the sheltered cabin, and she lay on the deck, clinging frantically to the rail and washed by the spray, as she made the long passage to shore, which she reached at last in safety, seasick and drenched with salt water. I met her soon after the adventure. She bewailed the utter ruin of her tailor-made

The Queen's Highway.

gown, but appeared not to be conscious of the danger she had courted and of her ludicrous position on the cabin roof.

The typhoon blew itself out at last and the sea became comparatively calm; the steam launch of the Grand Hotel landed our baggage and ourselves thankful that the journey was ended.

CHAPTER II.

AROUND TOKYO BAY.

Yokohama is the principal open port—there are six—in which foreigners are allowed to reside and pursue their varied callings. The others are Hakodate, Niigata, Ōsaka, Kōbe, and Nagasaki. At the custom-house wharf a polite official in blue European dress and gold buttons opened and examined our baggage carefully, and then strapped it up again—but one instance of the many civilities shown us in Japan.

The inspection over, we were besieged by crowds of jinrickisha runners. These men are short and lean, but splendid specimens of muscular development. They wear short tights of blue cotton cloth, overshirts of the same material open at the neck, with wide, hanging sleeves. A strip of cotton is knotted about the forehead, and when the sun is hot they tie on their heads huge mushroom-shaped hats of straw. Straw sandals (waraji), with a loop for the great toe and tied on by twists of straw, complete the dress. The sandals are quickly worn out and easily replaced, as they cost but two sen a pair. As the roads are perfectly hard and smooth, the coolies trot along easily at the rate of five miles an hour, making on level roads thirty miles a day. In going up hill or on long journeys, a second coolie (atoshi) is required. At night they carry small

YOKOHAMA BAY FROM "THE BLUFF."

Around Tokyo Bay.

paper lanterns that "wink and darkle" like fire-flies. The "rickshaw" (an abbreviated term used by foreigners) was invented about 1870 by an American missionary, and at once became the popular conveyance. I shall use the more euphonious Japanese name of kuruma for the carriage and kurumaya for the runner. The kuruma resembles a large-sized baby-carriage, and has two wheels, a pair of shafts, an oiled-paper hood, and a cushioned seat with a receptacle underneath for parcels. The black-lacquered body is usually without ornament; but occasionally one is seen richly decorated and upholstered in velvet. In case of rain, the hood is put up and a lap-covering of oiled paper is drawn over the occupant, who is then securely protected. The hood serves also as a shield from the fierce rays of the sun. I stepped into a little carriage, the coolie raised the shafts and started off on a lively trot along the water-front, known as "the Bund." My first sensation was one of real delight to be on land after days of incessant tossing on rough waters; and the second, the novel experience of riding behind a peculiar horse with a swift pair of brown legs. The latter amused me so greatly, I had scarcely recovered my composure when set down at the Grand Hotel. My friends met me at the entrance, and I was soon located in cheerful quarters overlooking the bay. The harbor viewed from the veranda presented a busy appearance, crowded with men-of-war and merchant ships bearing flags of foreign powers, Japanese steamers, and picturesque junks and sampans, and stretching far out toward the horizon were countless fishing-boats with white sails made of strips of cotton cloth loosely laced together.

In Bamboo Lands.

The weather was so warm it was delightful to sit on the wide balcony after dinner with groups of merry tourists, while the band played pleasing airs, jugglers performed clever feats on the lawn, kurumas with lanterns tossing a variable light glimmered up and down the avenue, and thousands of lights in the harbor added brilliancy to the scene. Every morning I went out on the rear porch, from which on a clear day Fujiyama, the most perfect mountain in Japan, is clearly visible, rising in sublime grandeur 12,365 feet from the plain. The superiority of this mountain is due to its isolation. Fujiyama is held by the Japanese in religious veneration; it furnishes an inspiration for artists, who never weary of depicting it, and you see its outline more or less defined on nearly every work of art.

Every evening I heard under my window the low plaintive sounds of the blind shampooers, an appeal for aid and protection as they grope about the streets with their long oak sticks. They form a guild by themselves, the number is very great, and they all carry a whistle. In Japan charity toward the blind is an institution; the government has set aside this profitable industry for the support of these poor sightless creatures, and a blind beggar is unknown. Shampooing, or massage, is a luxury all classes indulge in, and this dexterous manipulation of the skin and muscles for those suffering from nervous exhaustion is said to induce sleep when all other remedies have failed.

First of all we rode through the European town to our consulate, through which we applied for passports to travel in the interior, and then to the bank to get our money changed, where we were agreeably surprised to receive a premium of

A KURUMA.

Around Tokyo Bay.

thirty-eight per cent. on our gold. The "yen" of Japan is divided into one hundred "sen," and the "sen" into ten "rin" each; at par it corresponds to our dollar, but in recent years it has greatly depreciated in value. They have the free-silver system, and under that standard the wealth of the Japanese had already depreciated nearly forty per cent. The rin, of which it takes a thousand to make a yen, has a hole in the middle for convenience in stringing. The copper coins are called by foreigners "cash." The coinage consists of gold, silver, and copper; but the paper money, or satsu, is the most convenient medium in circulation. The Mexican silver dollar is the only foreign money that is current in Japan; it is the monetary unit throughout the far East. With our newly acquired wealth, we hurried to the native town that adjoins the European, riding through streets where everything was strange—the houses, the people, the costumes, even the sounds were all strange.

BLIND SHAMPOOER.

As we alighted before a small shop, the proprietor greeted us cordially with profound bows, accentuated by every member

In Bamboo Lands.

of the establishment. Japanese shops are never large—are scarcely more than little alcoves open to the street; the floors are raised two feet above the ground and highly polished or

THE ONE HUNDRED STEPS.

covered with fine matting. The goods, arranged on shelves and in cabinets, are invitingly exposed to view, and at night are stored away in fireproof warehouses. Behind the shop there is usually a garden with trees and flowers, a landscape in miniature, for flower culture among the Japanese is a labor of love. Rows of wooden clogs (geta) are seen in front of all

Around Tokyo Bay.

doors, as, upon entering, visitors are expected to remove their shoes. If you do not, you are requested to do so. It was so very inconvenient, with our buttoned boots, that we usually sat on the ledge and had the goods brought to us. We had been advised not to patronize these quaint little shops, but to wait until we reached the older cities, as those of Yokohama were poor as compared with those of Tōkyō and Kyōtō. But it was all too unfamiliar and odd; like most new arrivals, we fell victims to the curio-venders and returned to our hotel to regret our weakness and make new resolutions, to be kept until tempted again to break them. The large curio stores appear to be in the hands of men with a keen eye to profit, who, having retired from piracy at sea, pursue a like occupation on shore and are usually very successful.

The most picturesque part of the city is the locality known as "the Bluff," where the well-to-do foreigners have their residences. The ascent is by steep, winding roads; its avenues are lined with fine gardens in which handsome villas are half-hidden in a luxuriant growth of trees and flowering shrubs. From this height the view embraces the town and the whole port. There are also several florists' gardens, charmingly laid out and stocked with foreign and native plants, one of which is celebrated for peonies of a hundred varieties, and later in the year we saw there a magnificent display of chrysanthemums. A short distance farther on are three caves, said to have been the dwelling-place of the aborigines. They resembled an ordinary Indian dug-out minus the door.

Fujita, the oldest tea-house in Yokohama, and much fre-

In Bamboo Lands.

quented by foreigners, is reached by a steep stairway of one hundred steps. It stands on the Bluff and commands a fine view of Fujiyama, from which it derives its name. We climbed the steps and, while resting near a shrine, listened to the following tale, which proves that rash acts are not confined to the western world: In 1881, a Japanese circus rider and his daughter ascended these stairs on horseback, and the father rode down again standing on his head and holding an open fan by his feet. He had made a vow to ride up the steps of every shrine in each place that he visited, as a sign of earnestness in asking the gods to insure him success in business. Apparently the gods did not approve, as a fall headlong eventually terminated his career. The interior of the tea-house was one large room, which could be divided into smaller ones by drawing the sliding screens. The floor, like those of the shops, was raised two feet above the ground. While we examined an enormous book containing cards of visitors from every country, in various walks of life, dainty little maids served tea in small cups without handles. Among many distinguished names I saw that of Commodore Perry, the first visitor, followed by Admiral Putiatin, an ambassador of Russia, the Prince of Italy, the Prince of Wales' two sons, the Grand Duke of Russia, the Duke of Edinburgh, the Maharajah of Jeypor, and the Emperor of Brazil. During General Grant's travels in Japan in 1879, he twice attempted to ascend the steps, but strong winds and rain interposed on both occasions.

My passport came and proved to be an important document. Among other commands and instructions in the long list of

Around Tokyo Bay.

what to do and what to avoid, the "bearer is expected to behave in an orderly and conciliatory manner toward the Japanese authorities and people"; "to produce and exhibit his pass-

TEA-HOUSE.

port to any Japanese official who may demand to see it;" he "must obey all the local laws;" when "travelling in the interior" he is "not allowed to buy from, sell to, exchange, or make contracts with Japanese in any province;" he is "not allowed to permanently dwell in houses of the Japanese in the interior," or "shoot or hunt" beyond the treaty limits; "at

47

In Bamboo Lands.

hotels where they seek lodging travellers will show their passports to the hotel-keepers." The local laws forbid:

"Travelling at night in a carriage without a light.

"Attending a fire on horseback.

"Disregarding notices of 'No thoroughfare.'

"Rapid driving on narrow roads.

"Neglecting to pay ferry or bridge tolls.

"Injuring notice-boards, house-signs, and mile-posts.

"Scribbling on temples, shrines, or walls.

"Injuring crops, shrubs, trees, or plants on the road or in gardens.

"Trespassing on fields, enclosures, or game preserves.

"Lighting fires in woods or on hills or moors."

After a careful perusal it would appear that former visitors to Japan had left a bad record, or that the Japanese are a very suspicious race. Later, I discovered that the authorities had just cause for making these rules; that half-civilized travellers had been guilty of bawling out "Ohyo!" ("How are you?") to every one on the road, had startled tea-house nymphs, had kicked and slapped coolies, and stamped over white mats and polished floors in muddy boots, and had acted usually like mischievous monsters. The priests of one temple were forced to post this appeal: "Stranger, whosoever thou art and whatsoever be thy creed, when thou enterest this sanctuary, remember thou treadest upon ground hallowed by the worship of ages. This is the temple of Buddha and the gate of the eternal, and should therefore be entered with reverence."

It was late in the season to make the ascent of Fujiyama,

Around Tokyo Bay.

and our party had been cautioned as to the risk; but the indications pointed to settled weather, and we decided to attempt it. We made hasty preparation—providing ourselves with warm clothing, heavy shoes, and provisions necessary for the journey—and we started for Gotemba at the base of the mountains, three hours distant by rail. There we remained over night, engaging guides, coolies, and horses for the ascent of the morrow. Fujiyama with one grand sweep rises sublimely from the plain. Farm lands extend to a height of fifteen hundred feet; above that is a grassy moorland, and then begins the forest belt, reaching to six thousand feet. The last eruption occurred in 1708; but it still ranks as a volcano, as steam can be seen issuing from a crater near the summit. It may again prove mischievous. From end to end the country has no less than fifty-one active volcanoes. On the mountain-side, built for the accommodation of pilgrims, are a number of huts, in which tourists find grateful shelter when overtaken by the fierce storms of snow and wind that suddenly sweep down. To avoid staying over-night in one of these wretched places, we started long before daylight, riding up among pretty cultivated fields in the cool morning air, and were well on the moorland when the sun burst upon us, illuminating the sky and distant peaks with all the wonderful tints of pink and gold. It was a glorious sight, something to think of for the rest of one's life. Our faithful animals carefully picked their way along the rough trail as far as Tarōbō, where we bought staves and began the climb. We soon passed beyond the groves of hardy trees, above all vegetation, to the aerial ash-

In Bamboo Lands.

heap, gradually ascending the ancient pathway through rocky ravines and over volcanic deposits, of which much of the region is composed. It was a long, weary climb to the summit, which we reached without accident, but completely exhausted by the effort of struggling through loose cinders. The difficulties of high mountain climbing can be estimated only by those acquainted with it. It was much like the ascent of Vesuvius from the Pompeiian side. The first woman to make this ascent was a foreigner, Lady Parkes, in 1867, for Sengen, the goddess of Fujiyama, who "makes the blossoms of the trees to flower," was known to hate her own sex and to keep devils to fly away with such rash invaders. On the summit of the volcano, two and one-fourth miles above the sea, a stone hut has been erected for shelter; and there we rested while the guides prepared dinner. It was a glorious day on the peak, and we sat in the bright sunshine and looked down on a sea of clouds and golden mist. Suddenly the wind changed, the white clouds drifted away swiftly over the valley; we saw the plain at our feet and the distant ranges that from our aerie looked like foothills. Magnificent as were the cloud effects, we were well pleased to have them disperse to give us an unobstructed bird's-eye view, and we clapped our hands with joy at sight of the world at our feet. There seemed to be no limit to the vision. Stretching away in the distance could be seen the bays that outline the coast, mountain ranges rising one behind the other, the lakes which lie to the north, dark groves in the valley below, villages here and there, and rivers twining in and out like twisting cords of silver on their course to the sea.

Around Tokyo Bay.

Not far off yawned the summit of the immense crater, from which issued sulphurous vapor. We did not visit it, as the walk would have added greatly to our fatigue, and our curiosity in that respect had long since been gratified by the sublime spectacle of Kilauea. We left that hardship to bands of pil-

PILGRIMS TO FUJIYAMA.

grims, dressed in white, with long staves and big hats, that we met constantly, plodding along with languid steps. Although sliding down the ashes to the forest belt was more exciting than agreeable, it made the descent comparatively easy. There was but little snow on the mountain and that lay mostly in the deep gorges, but we found no flowers. We

In Bamboo Lands.

passed out of the forest just as the sun sank below the horizon in an ocean of molten gold. Such a wealth of color I have seldom seen—red, gold, blue, green, and violet mingled in lavish profusion. We rode down in the still air of evening to Gotemba, reaching it long after nightfall. The goddess Sengen must have favored us, for the weather was perfect, and her satellites, a certain gentleman and his retainers, presumed not to disturb us. The next morning we returned to Yokohama exhausted with the hardships that have to be endured in mountain climbing, and delighted with the adventure in spite of prophetic predictions. The trip was made against the wishes of our best friends, who had entreated us not to attempt what few men cared to undertake.

What most impressed me in my first ride around the city was the tall Chinaman—a striking figure, with that wonderful gravity that never deserts him; and when walking, or flying about in a kuruma drawn by a Japanese, he has an air of belonging to a superior race. With long, black, tightly braided queue reaching to the knees, rich overdress of brocade, and cap, trousers, and shoes of satin, his whole appearance indicates prosperity. He has the skill to acquire wealth and the ability to keep it. In the Hong-Kong and Shanghai Bank in Yokohama, with the exception of a few Europeans, all the clerks are Chinese. He is also the trusted clerk in mercantile houses and hotels, the money-changer and the *compradore*, or middleman, who arranges all business between the foreign merchant and the Japanese dealer. Shrewd, upright, practical men of business, the Chinese traders have won the respect of

A DASHI OR RELIGIOUS CAR.

Around Tokyo Bay.

all who have been brought into contact with them. A great deal has been said at the expense of "John Chinaman," but in Yokohama he is the ruling power in financial circles.

We suffered much from heat and humidity. There is something lacking in the atmosphere; and it is a curious fact that Americans, as a class, cannot reside for years in that climate without having their health seriously impaired. Although the air produces a lassitude which makes all exertion difficult, I enjoyed walking about the streets, as it was a better way to see the sights and exercise was a necessity. But the difficulty was to avoid the kurumayas, who cannot comprehend why foreigners walk just for the sake of walking, and despise them accordingly. They will follow pedestrians calling out "Rickshaw!" until the victim is well-nigh distracted; and when they turn back new-comers take up the cry. For peace' sake I yielded, solving the difficulty by hiring one to follow me in my wanderings, and rose to high rank in his estimation at a cost of eight sen an hour. The one I made a bargain with had been specially recommended for his good qualities and his knowledge of English. I opened negotiations by asking, "Do you speak English?" "Yes," he replied. "Who taught you?" "Yes!" with the greatest assurance.

A short distance from the hotel is a native street in which shows of all kinds flourish. Acrobats, athletes, jugglers, living statues, deformed animals and birds, trained monkeys, shooting-alleys where one can try his skill with bows eight feet long and arrows half the length, are a few of the innumerable attractions.

In Bamboo Lands.

Religious festivals in honor of some god are frequently held there, and one day we chanced upon a most curious sight. The narrow thoroughfare was gayly decorated with banners and bright-colored paper lanterns, and was thronged with pleasure-seekers of all ages. The centre of the attraction was the "Dashi," or religious car, a lofty erection that towered above the low two-story buildings. This structure was of heavy beams resting on solid wooden wheels; a temple-shaped roof supported by a framework of bamboo completed the car. Seated in it was an effigy of the god and a band of musicians, who scraped and pounded their instruments, which rent the air with infernal discords until the ear grew fatigued and sought relief. The decorations consisted of enormous lanterns of paper with strange devices, huge bunches of paper flowers, and minor details connected with the ceremonies. It was drawn along by people looking as pleased as children with new toys. These festivals seem doomed to disappear, particularly in cities, where the tall cars seriously interfere with the electric wires. Nothing, however, could afford more novelty than the orderly crowd, composed of happy old people, invariably respected and honored; the middle-aged and the youth surrounded by troops of children; and the infants strapped to their mother's backs, peeping about in a knowing way or sleeping in blissful unconsciousness. How any creature could sleep in that racket was beyond comprehension. The costumes were indescribable. The long, loose kimona, with flowing sleeves, is the national garment; but in many instances it had been so absurdly altered and abridged that, in the case of very young

MISSISSIPPI BAY.

Around Tokyo Bay.

children, it had dwindled to an amulet suspended about the waist by a string.

A favorite resort within five miles of Yokohama is Mississippi Bay, which derives its name from the flag-ship of Commodore Perry, who, with his squadron, anchored there in 1853. He arrived in Japan armed with credentials and a letter from President Filmore to the Shōgun "demanding the establishment of international relations." At that time the Mikado lived in retirement at Kyōtō, and the actual administration of affairs was in the hands of about thirty feudal lords, one of whom exercised an authority under the title of Shōgun or Tycoon. He found the nation opposed to foreigners; indeed the very sight of one incensed them. Perry, a born diplomat, believed that he was treating with the highest power in the land; but he gained his end, and succeeded, where so many others had failed, in opening two ports to American trade. This treaty, which changed the course of Japanese history, was signed in March, 1854. An American had opened Japan to the world During the religious controversies of the sixteenth century, "the monks said that Erasmus laid the egg and Luther hatched it." "Yes," said Erasmus, "but the egg I laid was a hen; and Luther hatched a game-cock."

In the late afternoon, on fine days, we frequently made this excursion, a lovely ride by kuruma, with two men. The roads all through Japan are the best I have ever seen—hard and smooth. The route lies over the Bluff and through a pretty valley of small farms so highly cultivated they looked like well-kept gardens. Threshing was going on with cheerful clamor,

In Bamboo Lands.

and companies of children lingered about watching the fun. The grain had been cut and laid on mats in the open spaces outside the barns, and men and women were hard at work separating the kernels with flails; another method is to place the stalks on bamboo frames and beat them. Leaving the valley, we crossed a high plateau and by a steep, winding hill reached the fishing hamlet of Tomioka on Mississippi Bay, noted for its good sea-bathing. Our favorite resting-place was the broad balcony of a small tea-house, on which we enjoyed the sunset and the inevitable cup of tea. Looking northward and eastward, across the expanse of the Bay, the view out to sea was charming. The whole neighborhood is wonderfully picturesque, a fair spot in a favored land. Under the high cliffs, whose steep sides are clothed with luxuriant vegetation, winds the narrow path by which we returned to town. The air was delightful, and the ride in the soft evening twilight, "sovereign of one peaceful hour," most satisfying to the senses. The latter half of the route is much travelled, and we met numbers of bullock carts, pack-horses, and persons on foot.

There is something exceedingly attractive in the Japanese women. We secured one as seamstress—a rather high-sounding title for a person who knew less about sewing than a Yankee child of five. All day long she squatted on a lounge, *à la* Oriental, and worked incessantly, wearing a thimble on her forefinger for ornament and with the others thrusting the needle laboriously through her work. We managed to keep her employed for several days, just for the novelty of having such a bewitching little creature to look at. Her head-dress

DAIBUTSU.

Around Tokyo Bay.

was remarkable. The shiny hair, as black as ebony, was drawn up and back into a stiff design that seemed almost to affect the shape of the eye. The hair, which is loaded with oil and bandolined to keep it in place, is dressed but once a week. This necessitates the use of the wooden pillow when sleeping, a block of curved wood on which the neck rests. It must be decidedly uncomfortable, and it is certainly frightfully suggestive of the ancient execution blocks seen in the Tower of London. Her expression was one of peaceful content, and her manner so shy and diffident as to be almost embarrassing, at times. She said nothing, accomplished nothing, and apparently the small brain that lived under that enormous coiffure thought nothing.

By invitation we visited the lacquer factory of Kobayashi, where most of the costly Yokohama lacquer-ware is produced. It was a ride of two miles across the city to the factory, which adjoins the proprietor's house. We walked through the fine garden, in which various cultivated flowers were observed—among which were some beautiful roses and many varieties of geraniums, and great plots of chrysanthemums not yet in blossom—to the long, low, ill-lighted building with floor of earth, in which a number of men and boys were at work on articles in all stages of completion. Mr. Kobayashi himself very kindly explained the process to us. The article to be lacquered is made either of wood or metal. Then a hempen cloth is drawn tightly over it and held in place by glue; then the successive coats of lacquer are applied, to the number of twelve, according to the finish required. After each coat is

In Bamboo Lands.

put on the article is placed in a damp, dark room, to be thoroughly dried and then highly polished before receiving another. The pattern in gold or silver is put on, before the last coat of transparent lacquer. It is a delicate and laborious process, and it would require months of study to become familiar with the art. The Oriental workman is usually engaged in the same calling that his ancestors for centuries have followed; so his skill is inherited as well as acquired. Both the art and the lacquer-tree from which the sap is extracted were introduced from China centuries ago. When first taken from the tree, the sap is of the color and consistency of cream and becomes dark by exposure to the air. It is an undoubted fact that lacquer dries most quickly in a damp, dark room. Lacquering upon wood, in which the Japanese excel all other nations, is considered the finest of all their arts. Lacquer is used for as many purposes as bamboo. It enriches the golden shrines of temples, the beautiful articles sold in the shops, and the small rice-bowl of the humblest coolie. It is largely exported as well. After we had carefully inspected the factory and its treasures, the owner, with great courtesy, invited us to enter his house. There we met his wife and daughters; tea and sweetmeats were brought in, ancient specimens of lacquer and bronze were exhibited, and altogether it was a visit long to be remembered with pleasure.

The vicinity of Yokohama is of singular beauty, and one very pleasant day we devoted to an excursion to Kamakura and Enoshima. We rode twenty miles by train to the station and there took kurumas for the sight-seeing. Kamakura was

ENOSHIMA.

Around Tokyo Bay.

the capital of the Shōguns from 1192 to the middle of the fifteenth century. During that period the city, with its population of one million, occupied the plain now covered with woods and rice-fields. It was captured and partially destroyed

SHRINE OF YORITOMO.

in 1333 by two Japanese warriors, Yoshisada and Ashikaga, the latter of whom founded a new Shōgunate dynasty (1338–1565). The great military generals of Japan called Shōguns virtually ruled the country for a period of seven hundred years, and the Mikados, mere figureheads, lived in seclusion at

In Bamboo Lands.

Kyōtō. This state of affairs lasted until the revolution of 1868. The Mikado's army was brilliantly successful, and the furious struggle resulted in the overthrow of the Shōgunate, the restoration of the Mikado to his ancestral rights, and the establishment of a constitutional form of government modelled upon the European. A short distance from the station is the temple of Hachiman, a deified hero worshipped as the god of war. It stands on a high plateau and is reached by flights of fifty-eight stone steps. Many of the trees that cluster about it are centuries old; one in particular, a noble ichō, twenty feet in circumference, growing to the left of the ascent, is said to be more than a thousand years old. The temple, simple in architecture, is enclosed by a square colonnade, in which are kept the sacred cars used on festival occasions. We were also shown a famous collection of religious and historical relics, among which were a number of ancient and curious fans. Fans have been universally used from prehistoric times; by warriors, priests in religious processions, courtiers, firemen, and every man, woman, and child in the kingdom. One of our party was engaged in

A FAN.

MOTOMACHI.

Around Tokyo Bay.

collecting material for a book on fans, lanterns, and kindred subjects. A volume could be written on fans exclusively; their history, their uses, and the numberless legends and tales connected with them. I leave the long and interesting narrative to her facile pen.

For the military of Japan this temple will always be a sacred place. Its treasury looks like an armory, so many are the weapons that have been placed here as thank-offerings. Some are very ancient and have been on the shelves of the temple for centuries. There is nowhere a finer collection of arms, and an inventory of the valuables that are stored in that shrine is a roll of the bravest soldiers of the realm.

Less than two miles farther on, the image of the Great Buddha stands in a grove. The first view from the approach is startling. At one period it was covered by a temple, long since destroyed by a tidal wave. This colossal image is composed of gold, silver, and copper bronze, forming a figure nearly fifty feet in height. The mouth is three feet two inches in width, and all the other parts are in corresponding proportion. The eyes are of pure gold. The figure, formed of bronze plates six feet in height, was cast on the spot. The head-dress, of snail-shells of bronze, is there to protect the holy head from the sun's rays—an offering of gratitude to Buddha for his love and care for animals of all kinds. The greatest Buddhas of the world are said to be in Japan. The one in the park at Nara is the largest, but this immense image is considered the best work of art. Buddha is represented in a sitting posture gazing over the plain—silent, calm,

In Bamboo Lands.

impenetrably mysterious. The sacred figure is hollow and contains a small shrine. As the door was opened for us to enter we passed in, examined the altar, and ascended by the stairs into the head, which is dark and the home of myriads of spiders; not a sound was to be heard in the dimly lighted interior, and we left it duly impressed by the unique equipment of the cranium. As it was customary to be photographed by the priests while sitting in the lap of Buddha, we were "honorably" pleased to climb up and sit on his "august" thumb during the process.

On an eminence commanding a fine view of the sea and in close proximity to the Daibutsu (Great Buddha) is the temple of Kwannon, the goddess of mercy. The dark interior, lighted by a few candles, gave us but an unsatisfactory idea of the wooden image of the goddess, thirty feet in height and lacquered and gilded. These temples and the shaded paths through the groves were in perfect order, clean and tidy, showing that the large number of priests who reside there do not neglect their duties. It was both novel and pleasant to wander about among the shrines, up and down the moss-grown steps of these temples of wood, as well preserved as if but a hundred years instead of a thousand had passed since their completion. We slipped into our little carriages and were soon on our way to Enoshima, five miles distant, riding along the seashore, ascending the headlands, where the maples already tinged with yellow heralded the approach of autumn, and descending again to the water's edge, where in recesses, sheltered within a shelter, hamlets clustered under the cliffs.

THE GRAND AVENUE.

Around Tokyo Bay.

At a tea-house under most trying circumstances we ate the lunch provided by our hotel. We sat on the floor-ledge, stifled by odors of frying grease, and gazed at by a swarm of dirty children; while the coolies a few feet distant bolted with marvellous rapidity huge quantities of boiled rice, dried fish, and pickled daikon, a huge radish and a favorite vegetable with the Japanese. Leaving the kurumas, we with our guides crossed the rudely constructed bridge that connects the island of Enoshima with the mainland, and walked up a steep, narrow street lined with shops, in which shells, corals, and other marine wonders are sold, the most attractive of which is the lovely glass rope sponge, whose shiny, silken coils are found on reefs at great depth. Our expectations were fully realized: the island is very beautiful. Its steep precipices, thickly grown with shrubs and ferns, rise abruptly from the rocky shore, and the high ground is covered with forests. The moss-grown steps and winding paths that lead up to every temple and little shrine among the groves were most alluring. While walking through the woods, we noticed many curious land-crabs with bright red bodies that made great haste to escape. Traditions and superstitions without end are connected with this island, which for ages has been sacred to Benten, the Buddhist goddess of luck. In 1182, her image was placed in a cave on the far side of the island, and there it is still worshipped. It was a wearisome walk of two miles, up and down long flights of steps, through streets lined with shops of harassing curio dealers, down to the shore, where we clambered along a rocky path some distance to the cave. The cavity is thirty feet high at the

In Bamboo Lands.

opening, three hundred and seventy-two feet in depth, and can be entered only at low tide. Attended by a priest with lighted candle, we walked along the narrow scaffolding to the extreme end, where, on a small altar in total darkness, stands the sacred image. As we emerged into daylight, the view from the interior across to the opposite shore was enchanting. Both going and returning, we were beset by divers of both sexes, who for a small coin will bring up shells from the deep sea; the rogues with high art secrete these about their persons before taking the leap.

The day was drawing to a close when we left the island, and recrossed the bridge wet with the rising tide. A ride of two miles brought us to the station of Fujisawa, where we took the train and reached Yokohama just as the sun, like a ball of polished gold, sank below the sea.

Yokohama is intersected by a system of canals on which a large part of the carrying-trade is done with sampans. We hired a native craft one day and were sculled for some distance; but the evil smells from open drains suggested fevers, and we left the boat in disgust. In landing, we found ourselves at the entrance of Motomachi, the most interesting street of the city. The small, low houses extended the entire length; the fronts were open, and in each some little patient industry was going on in full view. We found much pleasure in wandering among the shops and watching the tawny, slant-eyed, pleasant-faced people at work at their odd trades and handicrafts. Coopers, makers of idols, baskets, dolls, wooden pillows and clogs, straw hats, rain-coats and sandals, trifles of

THE BRONZE BELL.

Around Tokyo Bay.

bamboo and paper, and weavers of towels were all industriously at work. Besides these articles, books, paper, smoking and writing apparatus, cheap jewelry, ornamental hairpins,

A DAIKON VENDER.

switches of coarse black hair, and other articles of personal adornment were for sale. Confectionery and food had place too; and from the restaurants proceeded the most horrible smell imaginable, that of pickled daikon. This vegetable, which so strongly resembles our radish, is about two feet long and in its natural state is not offensive; but after it lies in brine

In Bamboo Lands.

for three months the odor becomes so awful that no foreigner can endure it. It is grown and used everywhere by the peasants and coolies, and serves to give piquancy to their otherwise tasteless food. You cannot mistake it.

A charming water excursion within easy reach of Yokohama is that to Yokusuka, where are located the government arsenal, drydocks, and shipyards. A ride of fifteen miles by steamer down the bay brought us to the busy spot. We spent a short hour looking about, but the place recalled a section of the Clyde, and we had not travelled all the way to Japan to look at old friends. The real attraction at Yokusuka is the grave of Will Adams, the first Englishman to visit the country. Arriving in 1600 as pilot of a Dutch trading-vessel, he was detained on account of his knowledge of ship-building and mathematics, and became a great favorite with the Shōgun; but he was never permitted to return to his wife and children in Kent. To alleviate his grief, he, like others of his guild, accumulated a second spouse, a Japanese, with whom he lived until his death, twenty years later. From the hilltop on which his grave stands the views over the land and the landlocked harbor are superb. The whole environment is most picturesque. The weather was lovely. September smiled, a smile that warmed the country-side with a touch of the dying summer. We returned by kuruma, riding leisurely along the network of farms and rice-fields, stopping frequently to visit shrines hidden among the trees, or at tea-houses to allow the coolies to rest. The charm of Japanese scenery is irresistible. We reached our hotel in the cool of the evening, and found a

THE TORII AND PAGODA.

Around Tokyo Bay.

note from our consul kindly apprising us that the fête of Ieyasu was at hand, which occurs at Nikkō but once a year and should be seen at any sacrifice. The same evening we visited a Japanese theatre, where the play begins at ten in the morning and lasts till ten at night. It was too Europeanized to be interesting.

CHAPTER III.

NIKKO AND THE NORTH.

WE travelled by rail to Nikkō, one hundred and eight miles to the north. Part of this line, the section of eighteen miles between Yokohama and Tōkyō, was the first bit of railroad constructed in Japan. It was built by foreign experts, who charged an exorbitant sum. As the track runs over a level country and labor is absurdly cheap, the government was not long in discovering the gigantic fraud, and since then it has built its own roads. Both for military and commercial purposes, Japan has constructed fifteen hundred miles of railroad and is constantly extending the lines. These roads are all narrow-gauge, about three feet wide, and organized on the English plan with first, second, and third class compartments. The stations are roomy and neat and provided with separate waiting-rooms for each class. All baggage except that carried by hand is weighed and sealed in Japanese hieroglyphics with the name of its destination. The officials are natives in European dress. The stations are thronged with passengers, who clatter along on wooden sandals and make a most deafening noise. Japanese shoes vary for the use. Wooden clogs are ordinarily worn, but straw sandals, costing a sen a pair, are used in walking or mountain climbing. A few men were dressed in ill-fitting

BRONZE LANTERNS.

Nikkō and the North.

coats and trousers, but generally they wore the kimona, topped by the utterly abominable derby, the only part of European dress that has become popular. The women without exception wore the native dress and protected their bare heads from the glare of the sunshine by holding a fan between them and the sun. In absence of a derby, the men used fans also. The natives are now becoming accustomed to glass, but at first the panes in railway-car windows had to be smeared with paint to prevent the passengers from poking their heads through. There is a general system of telegraph lines, and the wires extend twenty-five thousand miles.

The journey to Nikkō, the City of Temples, was full of interest, as the railway passes through the finest farming district in Japan. The country is beautifully broken, highly fertile, and cultivated like a garden. Not an inch of ground runs to waste; not a weed is to be seen. Superb groves of maples, elms, and beeches adorn the uplands, and tiny farms dotted with thatched roofs cover the continuous green plain. The fields are of all sizes, from a plot twenty feet square to an acre or more, and outlined by ditches in which the lotus is grown for food. It is a land of small things. The people, the country, the farms, the animals, the houses, the gardens, the carriages, and all the articles used in daily life are small. As one goes along one sees rice-fields, tea-plantations, orchards of fine fruit, excellent vineyards, and every kind of vegetable. The grape-vines rest on horizontal bamboo frames, and pear-trees even are trained on trellises.

It was harvest time, and great bunches of rice-straw hung

In Bamboo Lands.

on the trees and fences to dry, and hayricks crowded the tiny dooryards. The lovely green bamboo fringed the banks of streams or waved in great clumps on the hillsides, and flowers grew on the ridges between the rice-fields and in every available spot, even on the thatched roof-crests. The dwellings of the rich farmers were not unfrequently surrounded by tall hedges or high palisades, and only the deep-sloping roofs were visible, half-hidden among the trees. The train glided along until we reached Utsonomiya, where we engaged kurumas and two men from the clamoring crowd and started on the last stage of our journey, a long up-hill ride of twenty-five miles. The road we travelled is an ancient highway, bordered along its whole length by rows of magnificent cryptomerias (a variety of pine), which form a pleasant shade. These trees grow to a height of one hundred feet, reaching sixty feet before they begin to branch. They were planted by a nobleman as an offering to the great Shōguns who rest in bronze tombs on the sacred hills. It is estimated that one hundred thousand pilgrims travel this road each year to the shrines, and a grander approach could not have been devised. We encountered a few pack-horses and man-carts, and troops of people on foot on their way to take part in the coming festivities. Few houses were to be seen as we toiled slowly upward, and little by little I fell into a state of drowsiness, almost forgetting where I was or whither I was going. We mounted the steep street of Nikkō at the foot of the Nikkō-zan range of mountains, the site of the most gorgeous temples in the land. Nikkō, which lies in a lovely valley at an elevation of two thousand feet above the sea, is a

HOLY WATER CISTERN.

Nikko and the North.

favorite summer residence of foreigners on account of its cool mountain air, and we noticed many fine villas embowered in shrubbery. It was here that I had an unpleasant experience with my kurumayas, who proved to be runners for one hotel, while I had secured rooms at another. The rain was falling, my party in advance had turned off the road and disappeared around the corner, and the coolies sped straight ahead as fast as their legs could carry them, in spite of entreaties and cries of "Mate!" ("Stop). They were speedily brought to reason by vigorous strokes of my umbrella on their lightly clad shoulders. It was almost as exciting as an encounter with donkey-boys in Cairo. We alighted at the semi-European hotel and were received by little waiting-maids, who met us with a "smile well-bred," bowed any number of times to us, escorted us to seats, relieved us of wet wraps and umbrellas; and vanished. The climate is very rainy, and next day we needed the articles badly; failing to make our wants understood, we raided the back regions and found the lost garments hung up to dry among a medley of native *bric-à-brac*. One meets with more adventures and sees more that is laugh-worthy in Japan than in any country of which I have a knowledge. After the landlord had examined the passports and decided it was safe to receive us—we were gratified to find him so kindly disposed toward us—he ushered us into pleasant rooms opening on a veranda that commanded a fine view over the valley through which the river rushes. Grand old mountains, densely covered with wood, surrounded us, and the unique little village of Irimachi lay at our feet. Everything was lovely—the birds and grass

In Bamboo Lands.

and delicious temperature; and each day, returned from sightseeing, we gathered there to see the mountains illuminated by the last glow of sunset and to enjoy the freshly made tea and a brief siesta.

The morning after our arrival we made our first visit to the hillslope where the Shōguns Ieyasu and his grandson Iemitsu sleep in glory. A Shintō shrine of the ancient religion has existed here from the earliest ages, and a Buddhist since 716 A.D., at which time a temple was erected by the saint Shōdō Shōnin. Buddhism, which was introduced into the empire from China, wisely absorbed the primitive Shintō, but did not supplant it. This spot attained its greatest sanctity in 1617, when it became the resting-place of Ieyasu, who was deified by the Mikado as "Light of the East, great incarnation of Buddha." Ieyasu was first buried at Kunōzan in the south, and the shrines there erected in his honor furnished models for those at Nikkō. In 1617, his remains were interred in this beautiful spot. It must have been a magnificent burial. A vast number of priests in gorgeous robes, the imperial envoy, the living Shōgun, and a long train of noblemen with two-sworded retainers, followed the remains of the dead warrior up the grand avenue of cryptomerias to the mausoleum on the lonely hillside, where they were deposited with all the impressiveness of the gorgeous Buddhist ritual. There are several approaches to the temples, but the grand avenue begins at the sacred "Red Bridge," a wooden structure resting on stone piers and lacquered a deep red, making a strong contrast to the rich green of the pines. It is closed at both ends by gates,

GIFTS TO "OLD JAPAN."

Nikko and the North.

which are opened but once a year to allow the great annual procession to pass over it. The main avenue is terraced with stone and shaded by groves of cryptomerias that overhang the moss-grown embankments. Half-way up is a small belfry with an enormous sloping roof richly ornamented with bronze plates bearing the crest of Ieyasu, in which hangs a fine bronze bell. The method of ringing it is unique: a huge log of wood is suspended outside the bell at such an angle that when pulled out it will on the rebound strike the bell on a certain spot, making a fine, clear tone that can be heard at a great distance. At the summit, where the avenue divides, is a massive granite torii, a symbol of Shintōism, twenty-seven and one-half feet in height; and to the left is a graceful five-storied pagoda rising, tier on tier of lessening stories, to a height of one hundred and four feet. The eaves of the lower story are decorated with painted carvings of the twelve signs of the zodiac: the rat, ox, tiger, hare, dragon, serpent, horse, goat, ape, cock, dog, and pig. We walked on between rows of stone lanterns to the entrance of the grounds, where the priests sell tickets of admission. Provided with the quaint scraps of paper, we mounted the handsome stone steps and passed through the "Gate of the Two Kings," which still retains the name, although the original figures have been replaced by hideous images—monsters with huge ugly mouths, supposed to have power to frighten away demons. It might improve the landscape if they would perpetrate their special gift on each other. In the large paved courtyard stand three handsome buildings with sloping tiled roofs. Under the eaves of the largest are painted carv-

In Bamboo Lands.

ings of elephants, represented with the hind legs turned the wrong way. The work is attributed to the famous left-handed artist Hidari Jingorō, and is considered very artistic. Two of the buildings are treasure houses, in which are stored relics of Ieyasu and the numberless properties belonging to the temple. Arranged in rows about the court are one hundred and eighteen magnificent bronze lanterns with massive stone bases, placed there by noblemen in honor of Ieyasu and lighted on festive occasions. The stable, in which the sacred white pony is kept for the use of the god, is decorated with life-like carvings of monkeys, represented as covering their eyes, ears, and mouths with their hands. Stone slabs with the "blind monkey," the "deaf monkey," and the "dumb monkey" are noticed by the roadside in rural districts throughout Japan, the idea being that this unique trinity neither see, hear, nor speak any evil. They are known by the name of San-goku no saru. Near by is the famous holy-water cistern fashioned out of solid granite and supplied by the Shiraito, or "White Thread Cascade," on the mountain. The water overflows its sides so evenly, it seems to be almost a part of the stone itself. We passed under a fine bronze torii to the Kyōzō, a handsome building containing a complete collection of Buddhist scriptures. The combination of art, architecture, and rich coloring in this courtyard is a revelation of beauty. A pretty feature of the place is the soft tinkle of golden wind-bells that hang along the eaves. Still farther on, up another flight of steps, is a smaller court, partly enclosed by a stone balustrade. In this court, crowded with beautiful objects of marvellous workman-

YOMEIMON GATE.

Nikko and the North.

ship, we noticed particularly a bronze candelabrum, a gift of the King of Loochoo, a bell from the King of Korea, and a huge candlestick from Holland. "Old Japan" considered these three kingdoms her vassals. Dazzled with luxury, we ascended still another flight of steps to the wondrously beautiful two-storied Yōmeimon gate, ornate with lines of beauty, intricate traceries, graceful arabesques, and marvellous carvings of Chinese sages, groups of children, dragons' heads, and mythical beasts. The cloisters on either side are elaborately ornamented with showy carvings of flowers and birds painted in natural colors and harmonized with unsurpassed art. Passing through the gate, we entered a courtyard containing several buildings, one of which is reserved for the kagura, or sacred dance, of ancient date. The dancer was a priestess, also of ancient date. She wore wide trousers of silk, overdress of some light material, a wreath of artificial flowers, and alternately held in her hands fans or strings of bells. She postured and waved her gauzy mantle, made strange passes with fans and bells, while priests, squatted in a semicircle, beat drums and groaned hymns in unison. The music was melancholy and weird, the performance tedious and absurd. In another building we were shown the sacred cars used in religious processions and supposed to be occupied by the deities who are expected annually to grace the occasion.

In the centre of the court is the sacred enclosure, or holy of holies, containing the chapel, which we entered by the splendid Karamon gate, constructed of precious woods from China, beautifully inlaid with flowers and birds in relief, each

In Bamboo Lands.

finished with the same patient, loving care of decoration. We removed our foot-gear before treading on the moss-like mats of the antechamber, that have never been desecrated by barbarian boots. The walls and ceilings are lavishly ornamented with bronzes, carvings, frescoes, and gold and black lacquer. We gazed and wondered at the skill that arranged this harmonious coloring and luxuriance of decoration. Within the oratory there is neither furniture nor ornament, except the universal emblem of Shintōism, the gohei, solidly gilt and attached to a long wand (the ordinary one to be seen in every Shintō shrine is composed of twisted strips of gilt paper), and a black-lacquered table, on which stands a lonely Shintō mirror. The cool dimness of the interior and the atmosphere of antiquity remain indelibly impressed on my mind. We had exhausted our vocabulary and ourselves in admiration of these matchless shrines; yet all this splendor is but a prelude to the tomb itself, on the summit of the sacred hill. It is reached by returning to the courtyard, passing through an old doorway, over which is a famous carving of a sleeping cat, the *chef d'œuvre* of the left-handed artist Hidari Jingorō, and ascending two hundred and twenty moss-grown steps to the mausoleum, where rest the ashes of the greatest ruler Japan ever produced.

The tomb is of massive stone surmounted by a pagoda-shaped urn of the finest gold, silver and copper bronze. In front, on a low stone table, are a bronze incense-burner, a vase of bronze with lotus flowers and leaves in brass, and a bronze tortoise supporting a stork. This last-mentioned ornament is

GATE OF THE CHAPEL OF IEYASU.

Nikko and the North.

seen frequently in temples, and typifies " length of days." The enclosure is surmounted by a lofty stone wall with balustrade, and shaded by grand old cryptomerias and a luxuriant growth of azaleas and bamboo grass. This unadorned tomb of the mighty Shōgun standing in silence and in shade above and behind the splendid red-lacquered temples raised in his honor is a stately finish to this exquisite creation. We retraced our steps by the massive stairways gray with lichen, each stone fitted with such exactness, and without mortar, as to stand the wear and tear of nearly three centuries without displacement, down through the temple courts to the main avenue.

The temples of Iemitsu, in close proximity to those of Ieyasu, are reached by an avenue that branches from the grand approach. On the right are two temples of the Shintō faith, plain but of much interest. On the left is a red-lacquered building dedicated to Amida in which are preserved the bones of Yoritomo, the founder of the Shōgunate, a shrewd, unscrupulous, ambitious personage. A flight of steps leads to the entrance guarded on either side by two gigantic wooden figures painted a bright red and standing in niches. In the inner court we noticed a massive stone water-basin.

Another flight of steps brought us to the gate called Nitenmon, whose four handsomely finished niches are occupied by mythological figures of gods. Those of wind and thunder, making a great display of teeth, are the most absurd of the quartette. The coloring is intense.

Passing through the courtyard, we ascended successive flights of steps to the splendid Yashamon gate, the most beau-

In Bamboo Lands.

tiful of the series. The oratory and chapel are as magnificently decorated as those of Ieyasu, and brilliant with all the gorgeous paraphernalia of Buddhist worship. The temples of Ieyasu, dedicated in later years to Shintōism, have been shorn of ornaments, but those of Iemitsu still remain in Buddhist hands.

The bronze tomb, reached by ascending more flights of steps, is enclosed by high stone walls and shaded by a wealth of cryptomerias.

After seeing the tomb, we went by special permission to inspect the treasures in the Tamayu of Iemitsu. The iron storeroom contains a second smaller room, on whose walls are hung about twenty of the finest examples of decorative painting that could be achieved by the Japanese artists of the seventeenth century, working without the smallest concern for time or expense. The subjects depicted are all Buddhistic. Gold is profusely used, and used with a firmness, directness, and fineness of stroke that are absolutely marvellous. The colors are wonderfully rich and mellow; indeed, the best of the pictures seem to radiate a perfect glow of brilliancy, without, however, the slightest approach to garishness or obtrusiveness. The original silk on which the picture is painted is not suffered to appear at all, being completely covered with microscopic illumination or beautifully designed brocades in glorious colors. The borders, which in ordinary pictures consist of rich fabrics, are here replaced by hand-painting inconceivably accurate and minute. The artist, in fact, took a single piece of seamless silk, specially woven for the purpose, perhaps eight feet long

MOSS-GROWN STEPS TO THE TOMB. IEYASU.

Nikko and the North.

and four wide, and covered the entire surface with illuminated painting, from the elaborate borders of scrolls and diapers to the central deity clothed in raiment of gold cloth, every line of which is faithfully produced. In the same storeroom are many other objects of beauty and interest; for example, a number of illuminated scrolls enclosed in a lacquer case that is of itself a marvel; some boxes of the most exquisite filigree metal-work; and the norimono in which the mortuary tablet of Iemitsu was carried to the shrine."

All this gives but a faint idea of the magnificent care lavished by the men of old on the mausolea of their ancestors.

This aggregation of gates, bronze lanterns, superb temples and their rich contents, are fully equal to those of Ieyasu. No pen can adequately describe these glorious shrines in their deep green setting of cryptomerias, this expression of a racial genius, and all attempts must begin in utter despair and end in absolute failure. Nor can one compare them with that world-renowned temple-tomb of India, the Taj Mahal, for they have not a single detail in common. We remained a week at Nikkō and visited the temples each day, and each day became more enchanted.

The festival of Ieyasu took place as advertised. A slight shower had passed and the day was faultless. Midway up the grand avenue the hotel had provided benches and refreshments, and there, toward noon, we assembled and waited. Soon with heaven-piercing shouts, a crowd of men and boys appeared, dragging a large pine-tree up the avenue and followed by a multitude of people eager to secure branchlets as

In Bamboo Lands.

charms against evil spirits. So great was their success that, upon reaching the summit, the stalk was bare. The echo of the shouts had scarcely died away when the grand entrance-gate was thrown open, and the religious procession was seen to leave the grounds and move down the avenue. If you wish to see something that will divert you, you should witness a festival of this nature. It was one of those pageants peculiar to Japan, a sort of religious masquerade, "like a reflection of the magnificence of the past; serving to remind the people of the traditions, the personages, and the illustrious events of early times." I expect never to see the like again. The procession approached with music and waving banners. At the head were priests, mounted on the sacred ponies and clothed in gold-brocaded robes, or in crimson silk chasubles and white cassocks, and followed by a retinue in bright-yellow gowns and black-lacquered caps, holding aloft huge temple fans on long poles that were curious and characteristic. Warriors, dressed and armed in the ancient style, played their part, too, in this fantastic show. Then came men and boys wearing masques and quaint costumes of three hundred years ago, belonging to the temple and worn only on festival days. They waved banners and curious flag-shaped ornaments used in temples; others carried live birds and monkeys, or walked in pairs, partly hidden under the skins of ferocious beasts. Scattered at intervals were the sacred cars, huge structures built on wooden wheels, with temple-like roofs, black-lacquered bodies, valances of rich needlework, gorgeous old draperies of red and yellow silk, and drawn along by strings of devotees. Bands of

TOMB OF IEYASU.

Nikko and the North.

music in the procession made a most horrible din with gongs and others with drums slung on a pole on which others banged; and scores of primitive flutes and fifes squeaked to bring out the noise with livelier intensity. There is no difficulty which may not be overcome by determination! The train was at least a mile in length, and along the avenue flowed an immense crowd, which had come from every part of the country to enjoy this celebrated festival. The procession marched slowly over the sacred "Red Bridge" and through the town, holding high carnival until evening. The fête lasted but one day, and closed that night with a grand illumination of the temples and grounds. Innumerable huge, gay-colored paper lanterns flashed light from every building and gateway, the pagoda, the trees that line the stairways to the tomb, and the tomb itself. Hundreds of bronze and stone lanterns added their quota of light; and the vast crowd carried small lighted lanterns of paper. The soft breeze swayed the golden windbells, and from the main avenue floated upward the deep tones of the great bronze bell. We walked up through this materialized fairyland to the summit of the hill and looked down the long green vista of the pines over the brilliantly lighted grounds. It was a sight rare and impressive—a beautiful spectacle, such as the Champs Elysées all *en fête*, one blaze of light, could not rival.

Nikkō and its environs have endless attractions. It has lofty mountains, deep valleys, cascades gliding down the hillsides and foaming over rocks; frolicsome little rivulets scatter through the beautiful groves, and the paths and dells are endless.

In Bamboo Lands.

Our favorite walk was along the sacred river, a clear mountain stream that rushes noisily between banks of mighty rocks. Arranged in a long row are hundreds of sacred images of Amida, a powerful deity who dwells in a lovely paradise to the west. These worn and moss-grown figures, roughly hewn from stone, have for ages contemplated the "sunny splendor" of that marvellous valley. It is difficult to describe the effect produced by them. It is said to be impossible to count these images, never twice alike, but we had reason to believe that this legend applies only to devout Buddhists. We don't know exactly how it was, but one day, while examining them closely, a head fell off and we sprang aside just in time to save our toes. After recovering sufficiently from the excitement, we reverently replaced it, that future visitors might miss none of the diversions.

Another pleasant walk was through the village street, where we spent hours in the shops, particularly those in which photographic views were sold. Every evening the hotel corridors were thronged with dealers in pretty curios and in articles made from skins and a black fossil wood from Sendai. We selected a few, which we purchased for much less than the price demanded. A Japanese can always buy of his countrymen for half the price which a foreigner is asked to pay, and even then, so cheap is skilled labor, the dealer makes a very satisfactory profit.

We made a day's excursion to lovely waterfalls in the vicinity. The abundant moisture of this locality covers the hills to their summits with pines, maples, bamboo, and wild azaleas in

YASHAMON GATE. IEMITSU.

Nikko and the North.

great profusion. It was a charming ride by kuruma around the base of Toyama to a tea-house that commands a fine view of Kirifuri-no-taki, or "The Mist-Falling Cascade." As soon as we alighted, attendants brought on lacquered trays tea (without sugar or milk), which we had learned to like, and sweetmeats that we thought insipid. We soon became accustomed to the bitter flavor of green tea, and it was well we did, as there are few countries where water is so dangerous to drink, without boiling. From the balcony we enjoyed watching the waterfall as it made its trial plunge and piled itself on the rocks below. On taking our departure we placed on the tray the expected small coin. For a nearer view, we walked along a steep, rough path to the foot of the cascade, which falls over a cliff carpeted with rare ferns and every species of moss, kept ever green by the spray, that can find foothold in the crevices of the rocks. Birds chirped overhead, and we lingered long in that secluded retreat of marvellous beauty.

A tramp of two miles through woods and densely shaded ravines, crossing and recrossing an erratic little stream of many bendings and aspects, brought us to Makura-no-taki, or the "Pillow Cascade," sixty feet in height. Picturesque as it is, it is not a paradise. Serpents lurk among the wild flowers and lie on the rocks, and one of a poisonous species that crawled leisurely across the path threw a barefooted coolie into paroxysms of fear.

From Nikkō it is usual to make an excursion to Lakes Chū-zenji and Yumoto, higher up in the mountains. Our choice of conveyance lay between saddle-horses with bad reputations for

In Bamboo Lands.

biting and kicking, and so small I should be averse to mounting one, and kagos, a kind of basket-chair, suspended on a strong bamboo pole and carried on the shoulders of two men. We chose the kago. The seat is very low and the position tiresome; but it is very much better suited to rough mountain trips than the more comfortable kuruma. Thus fitted out, we started. All the first part of the journey was a gradual ascent by a rough road with an abundance of shrubs and wild flowers growing by the wayside. There was plenty of dust and plenty of sun, until we entered a mountain gorge. Walls of basalt, a rock comparatively rare in Japan, loomed up on either side and a mountain torrent rushed down the valley. Leaving the kurumayas at a tea-house for rest and refreshment, we walked along the winding road which skirts the stream for a considerable distance, under cliffs from which water trickled on our heads, and crossed to the opposite shore by a frail bridge of bamboo. A little farther on we came unexpectedly to a stream that blocked the path, and were obliged to wait until the coolies arrived to carry us over. As we proceeded, the flowers that come in the autumn blazed in scarlet glory along the path; birds sat on the bushes and examined us, in no wise disturbed by our coming; an indescribable sweetness breathed around us. The zig-zag paths up the mountain were steep and slippery, but the views through the trees were sublime. As we crept higher and higher, to the left towered cloud-capped mountains rising height beyond height, broken at intervals by valleys densely wooded and tinted with the reds and yellows of early autumn. We could look down hundreds of feet and see

SACRED IMAGES OF AMIDA.

Nikko and the North.

tall trees that from that elevation resembled small shrubs. With hearts bursting with gladness, we fairly caught our breath at the beauty of the scene, and one of the party, a stolid German scientist, was roused to remark that the scenery equalled that of the Hartz mountains. A grove of pines, fringed with

LAKE CHUZENJI.

trailing mosses, covered the highland, and there we diverged a little to visit Kegon-no-taki, a magnificent waterfall that leaps three hundred and fifty feet to a rocky pool below. The volume of water was great after the summer rains, and we descended the steep precipice of two hundred feet bespattered with foam, regardless of the notice that the old, the young, or those who had had too much "sake" were not to go down.

In Bamboo Lands.

The owner of the "notice" showed us some very curious specimens of fossil and ossified woods. Chūzenji, so delightfully located on the lake, is very popular as a summer home among the wealthy Japanese, but its pretty tea-houses were nearly deserted at this season. Selecting one with a fine outlook over the lake, we ate our luncheon on the balcony and enjoyed the extended views. The sacred mountain of Nantaisan rises abruptly ten thousand feet from the east shore and low hills covered with trees enclose the other side, all charmingly reflected on the unruffled water. There are many celebrated mountains in this district, each with its own shrine dedicated to some special god. The wind god is supposed to dwell on Nantaisan, and thousands of pilgrims ascend it in the spring to a shrine on the summit. These pilgrimages have no flavor of penitence; they are made to conciliate his godship and keep him in good humor until harvest is passed. After a short rest, while waiting for boats to cross the lake, we visited a large red-lacquered temple, with black torii, a very sacred place. As we glided over the waters, which teemed with fish, we saw numbers of boats with fine catches. Our coolies and kagos met us at the landing-place and we were soon on our way, riding through groves of pine, elm, oak, beach, chestnut, maple, and a luxuriant growth of grapevines, azaleas, syringa, bamboo grass, and flowering shrubs whose names we had not time to learn. We made a steep ascent, and crossed several streams, visiting on the way the Ryūzu-ga taki, or "Dragon's Head Cascade," a series of small falls "dancing high and dancing low" that form two streams. We passed over a famous

A KAGO.

Nikko and the North.

battle-field of early times, and then, rising gradually toward the hills, we entered the woods. The foot-path grew less and less distinct; the trees were changing in character and appearance; oaks began to straggle along the highway, and pines became more abundant. By a steep mountain road we reached Yumoto Lake, entirely surrounded by heavily timbered mountains that throw their dark shadows over its deep green waters. The village, a favorite watering-place, five thousand feet above sea-level, clings to the base of the mountain as if fearful of being crowded into the lake. Here are numerous warm sulphur springs, that attract victims of rheumatism and skin diseases. Until recently the public bath-house was a feature of Japan, and these bathing places, open to the street, are frequented by both sexes promiscuously. This custom of bathing has been abolished in cities, but here it is still continued. The climate is hot in summer and cold in winter, and snow lies to a depth of ten feet, making the place inaccessible. The town is composed of inns and tea-houses; the owners cover these with coarse matting in the fall, and escape the frost by going to the low country to remain until spring.

We had intended to return to Chūzenji that night, but a typhoon rain came on that turned the streams into torrents and the roads into mud-holes, making it unsafe to travel. One who has experienced sub-tropical storms will understand how masterful they are. The semi-foreign hotels were crowded, and we were obliged to seek rooms at a native inn. As we alighted, the servants fell on their faces at our feet, all the while drawing in their breath in a curious faint whistle, a

In Bamboo Lands.

polite way of expressing absolute submission to our wishes. The highly polished floors were immaculately neat, so neat that a lady dressed for a ball could have wandered about that house without getting an atom of dust on her spotless attire. The dinner, served on small lacquer trays, consisted of soups, raw and dried fish, tasteless vegetables, boiled rice and tea. Hungry as we were, we could not eat the strange food. After some delay the obliging landlord managed to provide us with fresh eggs, and with the addition of the rice and tea we made an abundant meal. The inn was lighted by the flame of a wick floating in a cup of cocoanut oil, placed in a paper lantern. My bedroom light, although more pretentious, only served to make the evening more dismal. It was a smoking candle of vegetable wax, stuck on an antique candlestick of bronze. The room had absolutely no furniture—nothing but the three futons (cotton quilts), on the floor, on which I slept with my down pillow for a head-rest. The wooden execution block used by the natives did not suggest comfort, and my dishevelled condition rendered one unnecessary. That night I realized, more than ever, how far away I was from home. I have no idea how long I lay awake, but it must have been near daylight when some small unknown object ran staggering across my face. I felt suspicious, but did not disturb it, and upon inquiry learned "it was only a centipede" with its numerous feet and length of four inches. Imagine my feelings! The bare remembrance of the incident tortures me, and no amount of travel can accustom me to these venomous creatures. The Japanese mode of sleeping has some serious drawbacks.

A CASCADE.

Nikko and the North.

In the morning, a fat little waitress brought water in lacquered bowls and pretty blue cotton towels for our ablutions, and we completed our toilet under the embarrassing stare of half the household peeping through holes in the paper screens. After an early breakfast, a second edition of our dinner, we made a tour of the town and enjoyed a row on the lake as the beautiful sun rose above the eastern mountain-top.

SALUTATION.

As we returned to Nikkō, stopping for lunch at Chūzenji, the country looked lovely; the air was cool and sweet, but the heavy fall of rain that had laid the dust had also furrowed the roads, making them in places well-nigh impassable. The waterfalls were lovelier than ever, and we could not resist a second visit. Arrived at our hotel, the same little maids took charge of our mud-splashed garments; but we had no difficulty in recovering them, we knew their hiding-place.

In Bamboo Lands.

The charms of Nikkō were so great we spent one more day among its beautiful shrines, so full of historic interest. That sky, those temples, those groves and walks, that charming combination of Nature and Art—it is not, I think, until you have paid them several visits and have gazed at them from within and from without that you become in sympathy with the very Soul of the place.

From Nikkō we went to the north. The following morning we rode down the ancient avenue to Utsonomiya, where we took the train and made a hurried trip to Hakodate, on the island of Yezo. Our route lay among rice-fields and tea-plantations, where we saw young girls gathering the leaves to be placed on mats to dry. Signs of silk culture began to appear, and soon we reached Fukushima, a very busy place, the centre of the trade in raw silk and silkworms' eggs. Silk culture is an occupation peculiarly suited to women, as it requires great care and delicacy of touch. It is carried on wherever the mulberry-tree will grow. We noticed groves of these trees and women in the house-fronts stripping leaves and reeling silk, and white and yellow cocoons lying on mats in the sun to kill the chrysalides. The hatching of the eggs is a delicate and laborious process, requiring constant attention day and night for three weeks.

The lacquer-tree, resembling the ash, from which the varnish is made, and producing oil and vegetable wax, grows abundantly throughout this region.

The camphor-tree also abounds. It is an evergreen, of the laurel family, having glossy leaves and bearing clusters of yel-

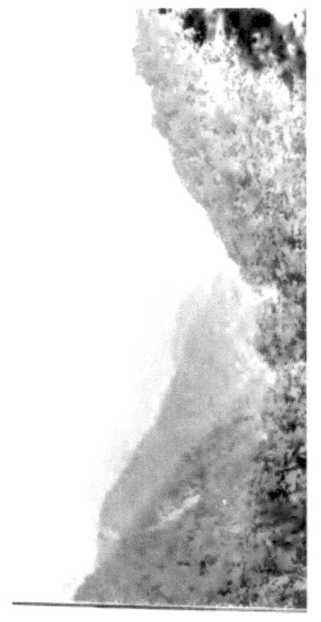

9

Nikko and the North.

lowish flowers which are succeeded by bunches of small fruit. The camphor is obtained by cutting the wood into chips, which are steeped in water or exposed to steam in a rude wooden still protected from the fire by a coating of clay, until the camphor is extracted and the gum is formed.

AINOS OF YEZO.

From Sendai, where we spent a day in visiting its famous castle and the temples, we journeyed among some of the finest scenery on the island, not unlike that of Switzerland. Few places in the world, for ruggedness of beauty and picturesqueness of scenery, can compare with these provinces. It makes an indelible impression on the ardent lover of nature. The

In Bamboo Lands.

mountains rise into grand peaks; the rich, warm valleys are highly cultivated; and the beautiful, clear blue sky is suited to the appearance of the country. There were few signs of life in the remote places, with the exception of the lonely charcoal-burners and wood-cutters, whose scattered huts and smoulder-

JAPANESE JUNK.

ing fires dot the forest. Just before reaching Aomori, the mountains gradually lessened in height, and we caught picturesque views of the coast as we speeded along the hillsides, sparsely wooded with pines and dwarf bamboo.

By a small steamer, we made the rough passage of seventy miles across Tsugaru Strait to Hakodate, one of the first two

YUMOTO SPRINGS.

Nikko and the North.

ports opened to American trade. The chief port of Yezo, it has a magnificent harbor protected on the south by a rocky cliff eleven hundred and fifty-seven feet in height, at the base of which the town clusters. It is a great resort of invalids, on account of the invigorating climate. Our two days were devoted to walks about the place and a visit to the museum, in which are relics of the stone age and a large collection of birds and shells. We saw there also several Ainos, who are probably the aborigines, if any still exist, and some interesting specimens of their work. They inhabit a province around Volcano Bay, a little farther to the north. The Ainos differ in character from the Japanese, quite as much as in form and in color. As a whole they are broader; they are darker in complexion, have heavy growths of hair and beard, and entirely distinct customs, religion, and habits. That evening we had a sail around the bay on a junk, in general appearance much like the Spanish caravel that Columbus commanded on his adventurous voyage in 1492. With the exception of the two great goggle-eyes on either side of the bow, the wood is never painted, but is kept clean by constant scraping. The large square sail looks awkward and is difficult to control. In the light breeze we wobbled about the harbor, much interested in the antique carvings and fastenings of bronze or of copper that adorned the stern, and in watching the sailors manage the ship. The native craft can be recommended neither to persons inclined to seasickness nor to those in haste to reach their destination. Myriads of strange looking sea-fowl clouded the sky and flew screaming overhead. Hakodate and the coast in

In Bamboo Lands.

general abound in a species of fish-hawk that utters a wild, shrill cry as it swoops down on its prey.

The next day we started down the coast by steamer, and for once the Pacific behaved well and the trip was delightful. We had fine views of the shore and the sacred island of Kinkwazen, near Sendai, and sailing up the bay to Yokohama, the glorious cone of Fujiyama suddenly shone forth to greet us, then as suddenly vanished.

A JAPANESE HOUSE BOAT.

CHAPTER IV.

TOKYO.

In 1590 Tōkyō, then called Yedo, became the military capital of Japan, the seat of the Shōgunate, and the Mikado lived in retirement in his capital at Kyōtō. Successive dynasties of Shōguns occupied "The Castle," which is strongly fortified by ramparts and moats. The Daimyōs, feudal nobles, lived in yashikis, walled enclosures also surrounded by moats, in which they were compelled to reside with their two-sworded retainers during half the year. The remaining months were spent on their country estates, where they lived in almost regal splendor. After the fall of the Shōgunate, in 1868, the Mikado moved his residence to Tōkyō and it became the capital of the realm. These sashed and girded peers were deprived of power; their estates were confiscated; their pampered retainers scattered throughout the land, and their yashikis, which occupy the northern and southern quarters of the city, are fast falling to decay.

Tōkyō, well situated on the shores of a fine bay, has no walls and no apparent boundary. Freight brought to the city is distributed by means of the artificial waterways; the main canals have a width of three hundred feet; the smallest are not more than thirty feet in breadth. The pleasure barges or

In Bamboo Lands.

house-boats of the wealthy Japanese are furnished in a simple, refined manner. As they glide along the canals in summer's time, a glimpse may be had of the sweet, cool interiors, from which issue sounds of the samisen as a woman touches the strings.

Architecturally the town is typical. Earthquakes are frequent in Japan, and that fact must be taken into account in all building operations. Miles of one-story houses with gray roofs stretch in every direction, and structures with two full stories are few.

During our stay in the city we lodged with a kind English lady, who occupied a small house of Japanese architecture close to one of these feudal mansions of old walls and crumbling towers. Japanese houses have a grace peculiar to themselves. Our pretty retreat stood in a garden, separated from the street by a lattice of bamboo and shaded by graceful trees and vine-covered arbors. The flowers were lovely. The trim little borders, the roses and other varieties that bloomed in profusion, all breathed forth a welcome. The house, very simple in construction, consisted of a light framework of bamboo covering about thirty square feet of ground. There is no foundation or cellar to the Japanese building. A veranda, shaded by wistaria, extended across the rear, and a great cherry-tree that grew near the entrance hung over the house like a shield. In warm weather the front was left open during the day, at night it was closed by semi-transparent screens of rice paper. In cold or inclement weather a second screen of wood is used. The interior was not divided by walls, but each floor could be

THE FIRE DEPARTMENT.

Tokyo.

made into one or many rooms by drawing the fusuma (sliding screens) that run in grooves at the top and bottom. There is one advantage in these movable walls: by drawing the frames you can enter or leave a room at any point you choose. I never knew how uncomfortable stairs could be made until I went to Japan. They were so steep and so highly polished, a toboggan would have simplified the descent. My own apartment was so small, I could scarcely move about in it without injuring the decorated panels; once I thoughtlessly leaned against one and made an unceremonious passage into the room next mine, much to my chagrin and to the amusement of my neighbor. The furniture of the house and the cuisine were English; the cook and waitress were natives with the euphonious names of Blossom and Spring. It is no compliment in Japan to name a child after an elder. Girls are commonly called Star, Cherry, Sunshine, or some such name, while a boy is Stone, Tiger, Bear, or the like. More ceremonious names are used among the nobility.

There amid charming surroundings we lived in comfort, without a care or worry except for danger from fire; the city has many times suffered from this terrible enemy, and in 1601 was laid in ashes. No people are more afraid of fire than the Japanese; for if a house happens to ignite, a whole street of these structures of wood and paper burns down with incredible rapidity. There is generally not much loss, however; for, as soon as a fire starts in a neighborhood, the residents quickly remove the screens, mats, and the few articles of furniture to a safe place, and only the roof and wooden frame are left for

In Bamboo Lands.

the fire fiend to destroy. So great is the danger that adjoining nearly every private house is found a "godown," a small fire-proof building with walls of mud or clay, in which are stored the family treasures.

Happening one evening to be in a distant part of the city, we witnessed a small fire and enjoyed a little sport watching the antics of the firemen, in full costume, with their antiquated hand-engines. Imagine firemen carrying a fan! but they do it, for I saw them, and huge ones, too.

Tōkyō has a population of one million five hundred thousand. Its "Castle" grounds, parks, palaces, temples, and dwellings cover an area of one hundred square miles, and the distances are immense. There are fifteen ku, or wards, thirteen hundred streets, and three hundred and twenty thousand houses. When a street passes through more than one ward, a second sequence of numbers is required; so there may be several buildings numbered three, ten, or forty, as the case may be, miles apart. A stranger in this labyrinth becomes hopelessly bewildered unless he has a trusty kurumaya, who the moment the address is given whirls his passenger up and down streets and short-cut lanes, and lands him at his destination without apparent effort. Owing to the vast extent of the city, we engaged kurumas for our stay, and every morning at the stated hour the faithful men were at the gate, with promptness highly commendable. We rode through the streets, determined on reaching the guide-book sights; but the shops proved so attractive we idled away many an hour, deriving much pleasure and some profit.

Tokyo.

All tourists in Japan contract the shopping fever, and a few suffer from it as long as they remain in the country. We convalesced slowly, and sustained a relapse in every new town which we visited.

The most interesting of all the religious structures in Tōkyō

SHIBA GATEWAY NO. 1.

are the Shiba temples, in which lie in state five Shōguns of the Tokugawa (Ieyasu) dynasty. In a grove of majestic trees, which serves as a public park, stand these temples, quite as rich in decoration as those at Nikkō but lacking their beauty of natural surroundings. The temples of the seventh and ninth

In Bamboo Lands.

Shōguns are the most splendid. We passed through the exquisitely ornamented entrance gate to a second, distinguished by immense dragons twisted about the pillars, and by the "Imperial Tablet" that hangs above the portal. In the court-yard stand two hundred and twelve magnificent bronze lanterns dating from 1716 A.D., gifts of noblemen to the Shōgun. By a third gateway we entered a gallery whose panels are gorgeously decorated with painted carvings of birds and flowers.

We took off our shoes, paid the admission fee, and, in charge of a priest with an intelligent, kindly face, entered the sanctum. It is a place of wondrous splendor. The interior decorations are magnificent. The three-leaved crest of the Shōgun adorns innumerable places, paintings of lions ornament the walls, blinds of bamboo and silk and hangings of fine needle-work conceal the altar. Small lacquered tables of rich design support lacquered boxes containing scrolls of Buddhist scripture. The three gorgeous shrines of gold-lacquer are said to enclose images presented by the Mikado and too sacred to be shown. The clergy eke out their insufficient salaries by the sale of a curio now and then. While in the oratory, the monk produced from his ample sleeve a piece of brocade cut from an ancient altar banner. I ventured to touch with profane hand the sacred fragment, and bought it for a silver piece—his soul and his silk for a yen! Of my part in the transaction I have yet to repent.

The tombs are of plain stone, resembling pagodas, and, like those at Nikkō, present a strong contrast to the grandeur of the temples. The shrine in the temple of the second Shōgun

SHIBA

Tokyo.

is of fine gold-lacquer, two hundred and fifty years old; the beautiful bronze incense-burner is of the same age. A short walk and we reached the Octagonal Hall that contains his tomb, the largest and finest specimen of gold-lacquer in the world. Hours were spent in examining these beautiful shrines, and at each subsequent visit we were more and more impressed by their magnificence.

Although the day was waning when our survey of Shiba had ended, we toiled wearily up one hundred stone steps to the summit of Atago for a fine view of the Bay. The scene was most pleasing; the sunset colors tinted the distant mountains and the white sails of junks that glided over its blue expanse. As we were returning, deep tones of temple bells came floating out of the narrow streets.

We spent a morning in the Kwan-Kōba, the finest bazaar in Tōkyō, a large low building in Shiba Park. The interior is divided by high partitions, and a continuous aisle runs back and forth across its entire length. All kinds of articles used by the Japanese in daily life are attractively arranged on its shelves; it was the best collection of its kind that we saw. The attendants were sweet little women in native dress—the kimona, a scanty, loose gown reaching to the feet and hollowed out at the neck, the large sleeves hanging to the knee, a broad obi (sash), and hair most elaborately arranged.

We noticed in the bazaar a Japanese lady robed in the latest Parisian fashion, showing the effects of foreign influence. In place of wooden clogs, a loose gown, and uncovered head, she wore high-heeled boots, a tight-fitting dress, and a much-

In Bamboo Lands.

bedecked hat. I shall never forget her indescribably grotesque figure as she posed with a self-conscious air, exactly like a dummy in a shop window. The sight was ugly and painful.

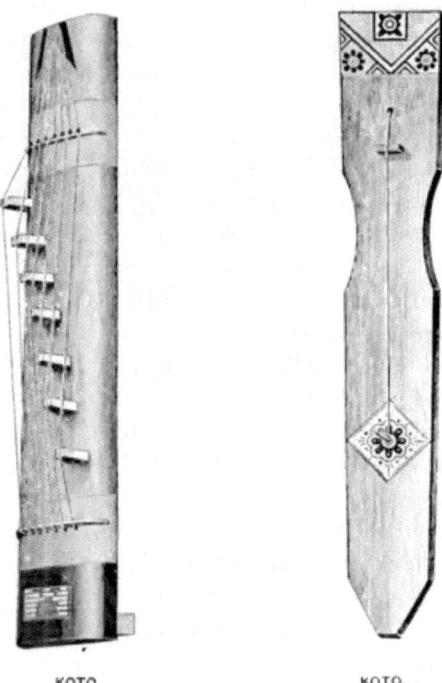

KOTO.　　　　　　　KOTO.

She must have been cruelly tortured by the restraint of her new costume, and I pitied her. No wise Japanese will lightly change the old for the new.

Tokyo.

Among my purchases was a small box containing four models of native musical instruments. One, the koto, has seven waxed-silk strings stretched over a sounding-board of hard wood and is played with ivory finger-tips. It is the most esteemed of modern instruments.

Another, a one-stringed koto, is very ancient, dating back fifteen hundred years.

The gekkin has four strings and resembles a guitar.

The samisen, the national instrument of the women, is not unlike a banjo.

The sounds produced by these instruments are agonizing to sensitive ears. An authority on Japan affirms that at certain Shintō festivals of great sanctity both stringed and wind instruments are played in silence. I did not attend a concert of that nature, but I could attest to its popularity with Europeans.

The Kōyō-Kwan (Tinted-Maple House) on the heights beyond Shiba is the most noted restaurant in Tōkyō, a resort of princes and nobles when they wish to give banquets. By invitation of a Japanese lawyer, we had dinner there—a dinner, a complete example of a native feast. The party, in addition to this gentleman, consisted of his wife and mother and three Americans. The Japanese were descendants of samurai, two-sworded retainers of feudal lords, and wore their mon, or crest, embroidered in silver on their garments. They were the first high-caste Japanese I had the honor of meeting, and I studied them. Our host, a lawyer and Harvard graduate, was well-looking in face, intelligent, and learned. No opinion is sought

In Bamboo Lands.

more eagerly than his, or more highly paid for. He wore a dark gray silk kimona, and attached to his belt was his pipe and tobacco-pouch.

The ladies also wore silk kimonas of sober tone; their sashes were rich and elegant, and in their head-dress of puffs and bow-knots were stuck costly ornaments of coral and gold.

GEKKIN.

The wife, so tiny she looked like a child, was very young, pretty, well educated, unassuming, unaspiring, with the most beautiful hands imaginable. Her face and neck were covered with powder and her glossy black *chevelure* was smoothed with great care. A Japanese lady never uses curling-tongs or crimping-pins, as it is considered a great misfortune to possess

152

Tokyo.

wavy hair; but if nature lavishes a large nose upon her she is always a reigning beauty.

Until the present Empress introduced a reform, married women were required to shave their eyebrows and blacken their teeth, as a wife is supposed to have attractions for her

SAMISEN.

husband only. This hideous practice amounts to positive inhumanity. The custom is dying out among the upper classes, and our friends were not thus disfigured. It is to be hoped that this, the first move in the right direction, will result eventually in the Asiatic wife attaining her rightful position in the household, as companion and counsellor of her husband.

Both ladies had that indescribable charm of person and

In Bamboo Lands.

grace of manner that seem to be the birthright of every Japanese woman.

The family all wore quaint little cotton socks with an arrangement like a glove-finger for the great toe; placed in a row at the entrance, to be put on when the party went out, were

INTERIOR OF JAPANESE HOUSE.

three sets of patrician lacquered clogs and three pairs of plebeian leather boots.

The architecture of the house was pure Japanese; the floors were highly polished and covered with soft white matting, which one would have been quite unwilling to walk on with coarse shoes, even if allowed to do so. The entire absence of furniture was not in accordance with our ideas of comfort.

DWARF TREES.

Tokyo.

The Japanese believe thoroughly in the "sublimity of space." The rooms were large; some were fourteen-mat rooms and one was a twenty-eight-mat room. These beautiful floor-coverings are made of rushes closely woven together, and are always of one size—three feet by six feet and two and one-half inches thick. It is usual to compute the area of a room by the number of its mats.

We first walked through the house, admiring its neatly finished interior. In the tokonomas, alcoves with highly polished floors slightly elevated, old distorted pine-trees were growing in ornamental pots; and kakemonos, painted or written scrolls of birds or landscapes, were hung on the toko walls. A Japanese interior is very effective because it always gives a work of art the advantage of ample room. The beautiful screens, the open-work friezes, the tobacco boxes, the sake bottles and cups, the soup and rice bowls were all decorated with maple-leaves either painted, carved, or of pierced woodwork. A veranda extended across the rear; from this we enjoyed a wide vista, embracing the curiously fanciful garden, the gray roofs, and stretching far out to sea. The garden was a miniature landscape; a pretty combination of mountain, lake, waterfall, dwarf shrubs, and carefully trained pines two hundred years old and only a foot high. A hedge was trimmed to simulate a huge rock very irregular in shape, and the effect was peculiar.

When dinner was anounced, we were ushered into a room whose only ornament was a large blue vase filled with chrysanthemums. On the floor were arranged six flat velvet cush-

In Bamboo Lands.

ions, and we took our places on them with more regard for comfort than for elegance of position.

The attendants were six young women in native dress.

The first course was served on trays; a small teapot, a tiny handleless cup, and a bowl of water were furnished to each member of the company, and the tea ceremony began. We drank to our host, then rinsed and refilled the cups, exchanging compliments in this way until all the guests had been thus honored. There are no large dishes; the plates are about the size of small tea saucers, the bowls of the smallest teacups; the teacups hold about as much as a wine-glass.

For the second course, before each person was placed a small wooden tray covered with paper; and, lying on it daintily, were a large round cake made of a red sweet bean covered with a kind of rice-flour paste and four sugar maple-leaves colored red and green to represent the natural leaves with botanical accuracy. The cake was nauseously sweet and the leaves were too pretty to destroy, but our Japanese friends ate theirs to the last crumb.

Sake, the only intoxicating liquor used by the Japanese, formed the third course. It is prepared from rice, contains eleven to seventeen per cent. of alcohol, has a faint taste of both beer and sherry, and is always taken before the real repast begins. The sake brewers, common to their class in other lands, are said to be very prosperous. It was served hot in long-nosed sake bottles and was drunk from china cups, which we rinsed in bowls called robiton, refilled, and exchanged with the other guests while drinking to our hosts and each other.

Tokyo.

If the visitors had imbibed the seductive beverage instead of merely sipping it, I fear one of the party would have succumbed to circumstances long before the ceremony was over. Japanese hospitality required too much of us.

The fourth course was a soup called shiru, made of salted beans, and served in small lacquer-bowls resting on tiny lacquered tables six inches high, called zen.

The fifth course was brought in on a plate covered with a second plate made of sticks of glass wired together. It consisted of oblong pieces of raw tai (the best fish of Japan), maguro (another species of fish), akajai (a red shell-fish), small slices of kyuri (cucumber), and our old enemy, the strong-smelling daikon. Instead of knife, fork, and spoon, two pretty chop-sticks of lacquered bamboo, scarcely thicker than a good-sized knitting-needle, from eight to ten inches long, were furnished. The natives use them with great skill, but practice is absolutely necessary. I could make but little progress with mine, and it was embarrassing, at a fashionable dinner, to struggle long with a dainty morsel and have the sticks slip apart at the critical moment.

While thus engaged, the wall in front of us suddenly vanished, disclosing another room, and the first dance began, called kōyōs-ōdōri, dance of the maple-leaves, a specialty of this restaurant. These geishas or professional dancers were of the highest class. They entered from an inner room, holding before their faces fans decorated with tinted maple leaves. They postured, twirled their fans, whirled on their toes, with many gestures, much pantomime, and an expression like that

In Bamboo Lands.

of the exquisite little Spangled Coquette that hovers over the flowers; keeping time to the music of the koto, samisen, and kokyū, an instrument played like a violin with a bow, while the musicians sang a low accompaniment. The music, which was considered very fine by the Japanese, was distressing to us.

JAPANESE MUSICIANS.

Their kimonas and obis were of silk crêpe beautifully embroidered, and one of the girls was extremely pretty. As they danced and postured, they looked as if they had just stepped off a fan or piece of pottery.

Then came the sixth course, of chestnuts, boiled and very sweet, fried anago (eel), snipe, a cake made of egg and sea-

Tokyo.

weed, stewed plums, and boiled fish with raw carp shredded very fine on top. A sauce called shoga, made of fermented wheat, beans, salt, vinegar and a dash of sake, was very good. It did not tend to make the raw fish more palatable to know that while one-half was being served to us, the dismembered carp was undoubtedly swimming about in a tub of water, as the Japanese always cut them up alive, and they will survive for hours if head and backbone are left intact.

The seventh course consisted of cooked fish, a kind of potato, preserved grapes, and a small piece of ginger.

The second dance was performed by one girl, alone. The dance was called dōjo-ji, and represented congratulations and rejoicings after a military victory. She wore first a handsome red silk crêpe kimona richly embroidered in gold, with a train that she managed beautifully. She represented children playing games, and at one time bent backward until her head reached half-way to the floor. The music was made by three samisens, the players singing an accompaniment in high falsetto tones. After posturing for a time in the red kimona, the dancer retired to the back part of the room, and with the assistance of another girl removed the gown and appeared in a lovely light-green robe exquisitely embroidered, with a girdle of rich silver brocade. During the dance this kimona was slipped off and a still handsomer one was seen, a gown that would make the Queen of Sheba envious. Her movements appeared graceful in these flowing garments, and she made good use of her long sleeves, which hung nearly to the floor; but without this drapery her dancing would have been stiff and

In Bamboo Lands.

unnatural. She moved not a muscle of her face, which might have been a mask, so perfect was the training.

For the eighth and last course we were served with gozen (rice), acmono (a kind of salad), brinjal (egg-plant), soup and tea.

The last dance came on during this course and was called

DANCING GIRLS.

gōnim bayashi, and like the first was performed by three girls. It represented a daimyōs' (noble) procession. Two of the girls bore lacquered toy norimons (palanquins) on their shoulders. In one corner of the room was a small tent made of red and white cloth (the national colors), which constituted the daimyōs' resting-place, and was decorated with cherry-blossoms. One girl carried a pole, from the ends of which

Tokyo.

hung little house-like objects representing baskets, in which the provisions for the noblemen were carried; a short sword was worn in her belt, but she did not draw it. The other two held battledores and shuttlecocks, and played an imaginary game which was very pretty and graceful. The names of the dancing girls were Moto (origin), Tome (prosperity), Seé (clear), Ai (love), and Masu (increase). The sliding screens that separated the rooms were readjusted at the conclusion of each dance—dances that our entertainers watched with every evidence of unqualified approval. Tobacco smoking, so universally indulged in by both sexes, was an important feature of the feast; from which, thanks to the courtesy of our host, we were excused. A tabako-bon, a wooden tray with fire-pot and ash-pot, stood at the side of each person. Their pipes, works of art, engraved and inlaid with silver and ivory, and enclosed in silken pouches, were carried in the breast pocket or belt. These straight silver tubes with a small bowl hold but a pinch of tobacco, which three whiffs exhaust. The tobacco is said to be almost tasteless.

The feast was over and we all arose, three of the party with pain and difficulty. This formal and prolonged dinner had lasted for three hours, and as conversation with the ladies was impossible, and we could not appreciate the strange food, the feast would have been wearisome in the extreme had there not been so large a share of comicality to enliven it.

The moment of departure came, congratulations were exchanged, we went down-stairs, and were rolled away in our little carriages which dashed swiftly homeward.

In Bamboo Lands.

Harakiri, thrusting a knife into one's abdomen, is an ancient and honorable mode of suicide, and sporadic cases occur to this day. For this they employ the time-honored instrument, the short sword. At Shinagawa, a suburb of Tōkyō, is a celebrated cemetery that contains the graves of "the Forty-Seven Rōnin," who dispatched themselves in this heroic manner. We visited the historic spot and paid our respects by purchasing incense from the priests and burning it on the tombs, where hundreds of former sticks had smouldered.

The following account of their exploits and death was written by the brilliant scholar, Mr. B. H. Chamberlain; it is better worth reading than any description of mine:

"Asano, Lord of Akō, while at Yedo in attendance on the Shōgun, was entrusted with the carrying out of one of the greatest state ceremonies of those times, nothing less than the reception and entertainment of an envoy from the Mikado. Now Asano was not so well versed in such matters as in the duties of a warrior. Accordingly he took counsel with another nobleman, named Kira, whose vast knowledge of ceremonies and court etiquette was equalled only by the meanness of his disposition. Resenting honest Asano's neglect to fee him for the information which he had grudgingly imparted, he twitted and jeered at him for a country lout unworthy the name of daimyō. At last, he actually went so far as to order Asano to bend down and fasten up his foot-gear for him. Asano, long-suffering though he was, could not brook such an insult. Drawing his sword, he slashed the insolent wretch in the face and would have made an end of him, had he not sought safety

Tokyo.

in flight. The palace—for this scene took place within the precincts of the palace—was of course soon in an uproar. Thus to degrade its majesty by a private brawl was a crime punishable with death and confiscation. Asano was condemned

OFFICIAL HARAKIRI.

to perform harakiri that very evening, his castle was forfeited, his family declared extinct, and all the members of his clan disbanded. In Japanese parlance they became rōnins, literally "wave-men," that is, wanderers, fellows without a lord and without a home. This was in the month of April, 1701.

"So far the first act. Act two is the vengeance. Ōishi Ku-

In Bamboo Lands.

ranosuke, the senior retainer of the dead daimyō, determines to revenge him, and consults with forty-six others of his most trusty fellow-lieges as to the ways and means. All are willing to lay down their lives in the attempt. The difficulty is to elude the vigilance of the government. For mark one curious point: the vendetta, though imperatively prescribed by custom, was forbidden by law, somewhat as duelling is in certain western countries. Not to take vengeance on an enemy involved social ostracism. On the other hand, to take it involved capital punishment. But not to take it was an idea which never entered the head of any chivalrous Japanese.

"After many secret consultations, it was determined among the rōnins that they should separate and dissemble. Several of them took to plying trades. They became carpenters, smiths, and merchants in various cities, by which means some of their number gained access to Kira's mansion and learned many of the intricacies of its corridors and gardens. Ōishi himself, the head of the faithful band, went to Kyōtō, where he plunged into a course of drunkenness and debauchery. He even discarded his wife and children. Thus was their enemy, to whom full reports of all these doings were brought by spies, lulled at last into complete security. Then suddenly, on the night of January 30, 1703, during a violent snow-storm, the attack was made. The forty-seven rōnins forced the gate of Kira's mansion, slew his retainers, and dragged forth the highborn but chicken-hearted wretch from an outhouse in which he had sought to hide himself behind a lot of firewood and char-

Tokyo.

coal. Respectfully, as befits a mere gentleman when addressing a great noble, the leader of the band requested Kira to perform harakiri, thus giving him the chance of dying by his own hand and so saving his honor. But Kira was afraid, and there was nothing for it but to kill him like the scoundrel that he was.

"That done, the little band formed in order and marched (day having now dawned) to the temple of Sengakuji, at the other end of the city. On their way thither, the people all flocked out to praise their doughty deed, a great daimyō whose palace they passed sent out refreshments to them with messages of sympathy, and at the temple they were received by the abbot in person. There they laid on their lord's grave, which stood in the temple grounds, the head of the enemy by whom he had been so grievously wronged. Then came the official sentence, condemning them all to commit harakiri. This they did separately, in the mansions of the various daimyōs to whose care they had been entrusted for the last few days of their lives, and then they also were buried in the same temple grounds, where their tombs can be seen to this day. The enthusiastic admiration of a whole people during two centuries has been the reward of their obedience to the ethical code of their time and country."

The Japanese love nature; they find in all her favors perfect pleasure and complete recreation. They show an appreciation, a love of flowers that no other nation displays; they cultivate the most beautiful, and bouquet making is a fine art. It is difficult to understand just how the Japanese see nature;

In Bamboo Lands.

for fond as they are of many varieties, they care little for the wild flowers that grow in profusion everywhere.

To see the floral beauties most esteemed and their festivals, one should remain in the country during an entire year.

TEMPLE OF KAMEIDO.

The plum begins blossoming in January and lasts until March, and is followed by the peach, cherry, primrose, pear, peony, wistaria, azalea, iris, convolvulus, lotus, chrysanthemum, and the tinted maple-leaves of autumn.

Tokyo.

The natives are ill-prepared for winter. Their houses, thinly built and insufficiently heated by charcoal braziers, are most uncomfortable during the short severe frost. When more warmth is required, they put on extra garments until they look like animated bundles. They retire early, as the evenings are dreary; a wick, floating in a cup of oil, furnishes but a faint light. The people hail the return of spring, and the whole population turns out many times in the year for no other purpose than to visit places which are noted for certain kinds of blossoms. We saw in the gardens of Kameido groves of plum-trees gnarled and drooping with the weight of three hundred winters. Crowds of people gather there in the spring to drink sake under the fragrant boughs, and to compose verses, which, written on paper, are hung on the branches as mementos of the visit.

The cherry-blossom has been called "the King of Flowers," and the "cherry-viewing," which takes place in April after the much-dreaded winter is passed, is one of the great flower festivals of the year. Then Ueno Park and its avenues, lined with cherry-trees in full blossom, is thronged with admiring crowds. Tea-houses, shops, and booths spring into being, to disappear when the holiday ends. They never weary of walking under the clouds of pink blossoms or of sipping cherry-flower water. The festivities last for two weeks. The tree-peony grows to immense size and its flowers reach perfection in April. In the garden of Yeiju-in is a peony one hundred years old and eight feet high that is considered a wonder, as much of the stalk withers in winter, leaving only an inch of new stem.

In Bamboo Lands.

The wistaria is seen best at Kameido, in June, where the ancient trellised vines bear clusters three feet in length and a single plant affords shade to a hundred people. The azaleas in the florists' gardens at Okabo are glorious in early May.

WISTARIA.

The "Iris-viewing" is a time of general rejoicing, and thousands resort to Hirikiri to gaze at the great ponds filled with iris of the loveliest colors. The river-boats, gay with flags and brilliant with lanterns at night, are covered with rush

Tōkyō.

mats, and pleasure-loving Tōkyō, bound to the iris gardens, picnics on the broad stream. The scenery is of surpassing beauty, and as the boat glides over the clear, unruffled water, the experience is one of quiet, elegant pleasure. This festival lasts but one week. At Shinobazu is a small lake noted for its lotus flowers, which in August scent the air. The castle moat is filled with them, and in Ueno Park there are acres of blooming plants.

In October, the chrysanthemum, the national flower, blooms; and then begins the greatest festival of the year. It is the finest display of its kind in the world, and is seen at its best in Tōkyō. The chrysanthemum receives undivided attention throughout the kingdom; the rich employ special gardeners to cultivate the plants in their parks, and the poor delight in purchasing them in pots for a few sen.

The most beautiful display is at Aoyama, the residence of the Empress-Dowager, and it was there by special favor we saw them in perfection. The flowers of every shade and color were enormous—triumphs of horticultural art. Some were grafted with half a dozen varieties, and others reduced to a single stem on which only one immense blossom was allowed to develop. The plants are cultivated very much as they are with us. In the florists' gardens at Dangozaka, which we visited in November, the flowers are arranged to represent human beings, mythological figures, trees, shops, castles, bridges, and peacocks with outspread tails. Flags of various colors adorned the enclosure, and as we entered an attendant came forward to explain the scenes on exhibition. The frames

In Bamboo Lands.

are made of bamboo, the chrysanthemums in pots are concealed behind them, and the flowers drawn through the openings and trained in shape. A few represented celebrated actors; the costumes were formed of chrysanthemums, and the faces and hands carved in wood and plastered.

Japan, always lovely, is very beautiful in the autumn. The natives love to view not only the flowers, but they delight in autumnal tints and flock to certain places to gaze at the maple and other leaves reddened by early frost. "Yamashime, the nymph of the mountains, is said to weave a variegated brocade" to cover her abode. Autumn leaves are named by poets "the brocades of Nature."

THE LOTUS POND. UENO PARK.

The most interesting month of winter is January. The New Year festival is officially observed, and every house has the pine and bamboo for exterior decorations, while flowering plum-trees, single or double blossomed, white or pink, trained into all sorts of odd shapes in blue porcelain pots or wooden boxes, make pretty the interior of each little home. The pine, being an evergreen, is a symbol of longevity. The bamboo is also an evergreen and represents length of life; the stalk has many joints, and the spaces between them are called yo,

Tokyo.

signifying age. It therefore "joins many ages in itself." The plum is a symbol of courage, strength, and virtue. Before the entrance gate of temples, on the last day of the year, the priests light great fires at sunset that are kept burning throughout the night, and children, each with a few feet of rope, push through the crowd to ignite one end at the sacred fire. If they can reach home with the light and keep it alive until morning, good fortune is assured for the coming year. This is not play, but a religious observance sanctioned by ages.

Ueno Park, lying on the northern boundary of Tōkyō, has other attractions besides its lovely flowers. We rode four miles across the town in a kuruma with two men—one to pull, the other to push—passing on the way a rickety tramroad with diminutive cars crowded with natives, and wretched-looking stages drawn by still more wretched-looking ponies. We ascended the cherry-lined avenue—unfortunately the trees were not in flower—to a point that overlooks the great city. To the west, we saw the cone of Fujiyama sharply outlined against the sky. Conspicuous among the miles of low houses were the castle, Shiba, and the long sloping roofs of temples standing in groves of pine, cedar, and bamboo, which alone saves the city from one monotonous variation of gloomy color.

The government buildings, of western architecture, displease the eye, and had absolutely no interest for us.

We continued the walk up the cherry-tree avenue, realizing how lovely it must be when the air is full of "pink clouds," hastily examined the minor attractions, and pushed on between rows of stone lanterns to the splendid gold gate presented by

In Bamboo Lands.

various nobles in 1651, as a memorial to Ieyasu. The carvings of dragons, birds, foliage, and the Tokugawa crest of three asarum leaves are fine specimens of the art. An ancient pagoda and a ruined temple are attractive features of the grounds. In 1867, Ueno was the scene of a battle between the Imperialists and the Shōgunalists, and many of its fine temples and libraries were destroyed by fire.

A little farther on is the Museum, a handsome building containing industrial, historical, and archeological departments and a valuable collection of national antiquities. One can there follow the life of a Japanese family through the whole course of a day. In one of the rooms are preserved specimens of the crosses used in the seventeenth century for the purpose of stamping out Christianity, introduced by St. Francis Xavier. In order to discover the converts, they resorted "to the infamous obligation of trampling on the cross." They are little plates of yellow copper, on which are represented in relief the instrument of punishment on which Christ died, and other sacred scenes.

Among the objects that most impressed me were some ancient images of clay. In connection with these antiquities it is related that in B.C. 2 the brother of the Mikado died; and "his attendants were buried alive round the tumulus in a standing position; for many days they died not; but day and night wept and cried. The Mikado, hearing the sound of their weeping, was sad and sorry in his heart and commanded all his ministers to devise some plan by which this custom, ancient though it was, should be discontinued for the future. Accordingly,

DAIBUTSU. UENO.

Tokyo.

when the Mikado died in A.D. 3, workers in clay were sent for to Izumo; who made images of men, horses, and various other things, which were set up round the grave instead of living beings."

On leaving that room and its uncanny contents I seemed to be awakening from some hideous dream.

Six Shōguns of the Tokugawa dynasty are buried here, and the temples and tombs, very like those at Shiba, are monuments of old Japanese art. Two hundred and sixty daimyōs dedicated to each tomb a pair of stone lanterns, and the courtyards are crowded with them.

When General and Mrs. Grant visited Japan, in 1879, they planted in Ueno Park two American cypresses as a lasting remembrance of their kindly reception and the friendship established between the two countries. They have grown large, and under their pendulous branches stands a handsome monument erected by the Japanese as a token of special regard for this distinguished American.

General Grant was welcomed royally. Tōkyō spent $50,000 in entertaining him, and the fête given in his honor in the grounds of the Engineering College was one of the most successful ever held in the capital—a veritable "Feast of Lanterns." General Grant expressed great admiration for the Japanese, and dwelt particularly upon the politeness and attention shown to old people.

"The treaty" made with the United States in 1854, followed by a revised one with all the foreign powers in 1869, has been a thorn in the side of Japan for twenty-five years. It

In Bamboo Lands.

opened "six ports to foreign trade," exempted "foreigners from the jurisdiction of Japanese law courts," provided for a "scale of import duties not to exceed five per cent," "the free exercise of the Christian religion," and assistance to "shipwrecked sailors." During the next decade Japanese students sent abroad to be educated returned with European ideas, resulting in a strong effort being made by the government to set aside this treaty so favorable to foreigners and frame a new one that would place the country on an equality with western powers. "Reform was in the air — reform, a dangerous change." The movement was most active with the young; the old conservative element objected strongly. The Japanese feared foreign emigration—the destruction of their national customs; her mines, her industries, her soil even might pass under foreign control, and excitement ran high. They clamored for everything foreign, and then clamored for the extinction of foreigners. The people broke loose and mischief was in the air. In the riots of 1889, Count Oŏkuma, Minister for Foreign Affairs, was brutally assaulted and lost a leg by the explosion of a dynamite bomb — showing unusual leniency in Japan, where complete annihilation is the rule. Now it seems probable that the new treaty concluded with the United States has settled the vexed question of "treaty revision" forever.

Our good fortune gained us admission to the residence of Count Oŏkuma, a large rambling house of pure Japanese architecture. No European furniture was allowed to disfigure the interior, and the gorgeous kakemonos that hung on the toko walls, where the art treasures of the family are exhibited, and

RESIDENCE OF COUNT OŌKUMA.

Tokyo.

the elaborate arrangements of flowers revealed infinite taste. With charming courtesy room after room was shown, all equally artistic. The Japanese are certainly the most courtly nation in the world. The house stood far back in grounds that covered several acres, laid out with the highest art; the whole formed a perfect exposition of Japanese landscape gardening. Grand old shade-trees, hillocks to simulate mountains, rocks with eccentric names, bridges placed for ornament over streams, dwarf pines and shrubs, garden seats and temple lanterns—every detail was pleasantly suggestive of art and perfectly adjusted to the plan of the garden. To make the spot really delightful, storks animated the miniature lakes, peacocks with outspread tails strutted the lawn, and flowers of brilliant colors bloomed in sweet confusion.

On our return we heard a great clatter of hoofs, and saw the Emperor and Empress coming. They were in plain European dress, and drove through the streets in a semi-open carriage, bowing to the right and left, and were followed by guards of honor splendidly mounted. The coachmen and footmen were dressed exactly like those of the German Emperor. Powdered hair and tall hats, dead-gold velvet waistcoats, gorgeous plush breeches, and flesh-colored stockings completed the livery. The Emperor and Empress are immensely popular at all times, and whenever they appear in public receive the most friendly greetings. The sight has its own fascination for those who do not mind a little dust—and none did. The Emperor boasts an unbroken descent of twenty-five centuries, and it is only a few years since his person was

In Bamboo Lands.

so sacred that few of his subjects ever saw him. Time has changed all that—and much for the better. Almost daily we rode along the avenues that skirt the castellated walls of the royal palace—closed to the public—and gazed longingly at the tall trees and tiled roofs of which we were to have a nearer view on the Mikado's birthday, November 3d.

Rain never prevented our going out. From my little carriage with hood drawn up and nearly concealed by an oiled-paper lap-robe, I could peep out at the coolies—clad in straw rain-coats and mushroom-shaped hats—and all the world, protected by cloaks of yellow oiled paper and oiled-paper umbrellas and perched on wooden clogs that add from two to four inches to their height. They appear to dislike damp feet and to enjoy wet legs. The streets have no curbs or sidewalks, and walking and riding are done on the same thoroughfare.

On bright days they were thronged with good-natured people, strolling bands of musicians, venders of toys and food; and occasionally we saw a festival car drawn along by strings of coolies, or a funeral procession with its cheerful-looking followers. Pedlers go about with long bamboo poles over the right shoulder, from which are suspended a set of shelves holding all manner of food and knick-knacks for sale. Frequently the way was blocked by bullock carts loaded with merchandise, or by coolies with pails or baskets carried on their shoulders. Children of all ages in abundance play on the roadways, with younger ones tied to their backs, and how they escape destruction only their guardian divinity knows. The streets that remain exclusively Japanese are lined with shops of small

Tokyo.

tradesmen, for here there is no leisure class—every one has something to sell. The shops stocked with European goods, shawls, handkerchiefs, stockings, stuffs for dresses, canned goods, derby hats, knitted garments, and worsted yarns, we

STREET DECORATIONS.

avoided. Before the entrance were women crocheting "Tam O'Shanters" and garments of startling shades. They were very much in earnest and worked hard to achieve a monstrosity. Toddlers with black beady eyes, bare legs, and with but a tuft of hair on top of the head, looked very comical in skin-tight

In Bamboo Lands.

jackets of brilliant colors, and precious cherubs waddled about perfectly nude, except for the amulet tied about the waist and a gorgeous "Tam" on the head.

We rarely saw a person in Western dress; except of course, the uniformed soldiers, students, or the police, young men wearing blue coats and caps with three bands of gold, who oc-

GAME OF SAI.

cupied the small kiosks at the street corners. The salary of a policeman is only about six yen a month. His duties are as light as his pay. I never saw a case of intoxication and never heard a profane word—for there are practically no oaths in the Japanese language.

There are more than eight hundred public bath-houses in

THE SUMIDA RIVER, NEAR TOKYO.

Tōkyō.

Tōkyō where for two sen a person can take a bath either hot or cold.

In the evening we frequently amused ourselves out of doors. Then thousands of lanterns are lighted. They dangle from kurumas, swing from the low roofs, glow in the open shop fronts, and flare in the flag-decked restaurants and tea-houses, from which issue the tinkling of samisen, the harsh notes of singing girls, and revelry of sake-drinking patrons.

It was also pleasant to wander among the torch-lit booths with the aimlessly happy multitude, or to follow a stream of pleasure-seekers to a theatre or gathering-place in the Ginza, where magic lanterns, singing, dancing, playing on the samisen were a few of the many attractions. The Japanese are a light-hearted, pleasure-loving people, and Tōkyō is the centre of amusement.

The first theatre in Japan was opened early in the seventeenth century, and for more than two years was attended only by the middle and lower classes. Recently one of a higher order has been inaugurated, that is patronized by the Mikado and the court.

One of the peculiarities of a Japanese theatre is the shape of the stage, which projects on one or both sides into the auditorium. This projection, called the "flower path," is used by the actors when representing some one starting on or returning from a journey. The main stage resting on rollers can be turned around, actors and all, when a change of scene is desired. The actors make the gestures and carry on the conversation, while persons concealed above the stage sing the chorus,

In Bamboo Lands.

accompanied by the samisen. This combination of discords and ear-piercing tones that issue from these sources is enough to drive a foreigner out of the place; and usually does. Women do not appear on the stage—their parts are taken by men trained for that purpose. When the play is about to begin, it is announced by rapping with a wooden hammer. The dramas usually presented are based upon some legendary romance or historical fact, like the story of the Forty-Seven Rōnin, and represent the manners, customs, and dress of "Old Japan." The comedies have a tendency to immorality and to corrupt the youth of the country. The plays usually last from morning until midnight, and the audience make preparations to attend the theatre as if they were going on a picnic, by taking baskets of food; there they partake of their meals with the same regularity as at home. The women are always seated by themselves. The most noted actor in Japan is Ichikawa Danjūrō, celebrated for his rare histrionic powers and his agility as a dancer. His ancestors for nine generations have pursued the same calling. We went to the Shintomi-za theatre one evening to see him in his best character. We employed an interpreter, secured a box overlooking the stage, and prepared to enjoy the performance. Alas! our guide was a failure as an expositor; but he scored amazing success in disposing of the lunch provided at his suggestion. Danjūrō appeared and, I suppose, played his part well, according to the Japanese standard; but the people furnished most of the entertainment for us. The pit was crowded by a more or less tearful audience, every member of which smoked a pipe. Between the acts

Tokyo.

servants from tea-houses appeared, bearing lacquered trays with tea, rice, hard-boiled eggs, sweetmeats, and fruit, that disappeared like magic. We remained several hours, notwithstanding the stifling fumes and the persecution of the music.

Some years ago an Italian opera troupe visited the country, and the manager of a Japanese theatre hired the company to sing before a native audience, who listened attentively and behaved with propriety, until "they had recovered from the first shock of surprise;" then they were seized with paroxysms of laughter at the high tones of the soprano. They "laughed at the absurdities of European singing until the tears rolled down their cheeks, and then they stuffed their sleeves into their mouths" in a vain effort to control themselves. The experiment was not repeated.

Public exhibitions of wrestling are given in structures of bamboo decorated with many-colored flags. We liked to watch the fat little fellows in their contests. We could have seats below on the ground, or could climb the steep ladder to benches reserved in the gallery; we took the latter, and looked down upon the performance. The wrestlers are called into the arena by a herald and enter from opposite sides. They wear nothing but an apron of satin or velvet, richly embroidered in gold with all manner of objects and bordered with a fringe reaching to the feet. Their hair, plaited in a knot, forms a tuft on their heads. The umpire, who bears in his hands a fan, stands at one end, and at the foot of each pillar sits a veteran wrestler as a judge of appeals. When a round is finished, the umpire lifts his fan on the winner's side, and if a discussion arises, the judges settle it. There are forty-eight prescribed devices in the art, each of which has eight minor divisions. These are not in accordance with Western scientific rules. The Kimura family monopolize the business, and a man who desires to become a wrestler must be a pupil of a Kimura and adopt the name.

WRESTLING.

The Buddhist temple of Ekōin is a noted place for wrestling matches in the spring and fall, when the combatants do their best to obtain promotion, and derives its only means of support from the crowds that flock there to witness these feats of skill.

Tokyo.

One morning was agreeably spent in the Arsenal and its extensive garden, larger and more beautiful even than that of Count Ōkuma, and another in the Yūshū-kwan, a museum of arms containing an interesting collection of old Japanese armor, swords and scabbards, and a few Korean relics. The

BOTANIC GARDENS.

following account of a street fight which occurred in 1864 was written by a native:

"The Choshiu troops were defended by armor, their leader clad in a suit of armor tied with grass-green silken strings, and covered with a garment of Yamato brocade. Over this he wore a surcoat of white gauze with figures drawn on it in

In Bamboo Lands.

black. He bestrode a charger, a baton of gold paper in his hand. Before him went flags and banners and two field-pieces, with a company of thirty spearmen. The spears, crossing each other, looked like a hedge of bamboo grass; bullets flew over his head like axle-trees. Helmets and cuirasses that had been cast away by their owners, spears, pikes, bows, and muskets, were lying about in quantities. A second leader was mounted on horseback, and held a baton of white paper in his hand. He wore a mantle of scarlet embroidered with his crest, the trefoil, and under it a suit of armor adorned with purple fastenings. His head-covering was a warrior's cap of bronze leather."

The hours flew in visits to markets for the sale of fruits, vegetables, and fish. A large portion of the population of Japan are engaged in the fishing industry; the waters are alive with schools of fish of all kinds, besides many other forms of marine life. The whole fishery represents a value of $20,000,000; the fresh-water catch alone amounts to $1,000,000. We liked to examine the pyramids of curious vegetables and the great variety of grotesque-looking monsters of the deep, and watch the traffic; and one day we made an interesting discovery in connection with it. After a selection is made the buyer resorts to a neighboring tea-house for refreshment, and there his purchases are brought for his inspection, and, if satisfactory, the goods are paid for and the bargain is concluded. With the exception of the mandarin orange, the fruits are almost tasteless. Not a few American varieties are being cultivated in the Land of the Rising Sun—especially apples, which

A WARRIOR IN FULL UNIFORM.

Tokyo.

are grown in large quantities in the island of Yezo for exportation.

There are no happier children in the world than the Japanese. Parents love their offspring tenderly, as one would conclude from the poetry they write on the appearance of each new tooth, and two days are set apart in the spring as festivals for them. The fête for girls occurs on the 3d of March, and every doll-shop in Tōkyō and other cities is gayly decorated and stocked with tiny models. Dolls are purchased and displayed in every little home; those stored away from previous anniversaries are brought out, and the morning is occupied in decorating the doll-stand, placed in the best room in the house. The miniature emperors and empresses are first put in places of highest honor on the top row, and court ladies in full dress, the bands of musicians, the prime ministers on the right and left; dolls representing mythical or historical personages, such as "the old couple of Takasago" or some great poetess, with a sprinkling of ordinary dolls. Musical instruments, flowers arranged in vases, paper lanterns, and other pretty articles are tastefully laid out at respectful distances from the august occupants of the throne above. This done, the girls are left to enjoy themselves, which they often do by having mock dinner-parties and other ceremonials. If there is a new-born daughter in the family, models of the Japanese court in ancient costumes—now never seen—are given to her on her first festival; if the family are in prosperous circumstances, tiny dinner services in porcelain and lacquer, work-boxes, and household utensils are brought, to be kept until her marriage, when they

In Bamboo Lands.

are sent to the house of the bridegroom. As there are no spinsters in Japan, the husband invariably gets the entire collection.

The festival for boys is celebrated on the 5th of May, and models of miniature warriors in full armor are purchased for the new-born son. A long bamboo pole, with a huge fish floating from the top, is set up before each little house, and is a most effective sign. It represents the carp swimming up a stream against the current, and is a symbol of the success a boy is expected to achieve in his struggles with the world.

Feasts are given on both occasions, much rejoicing is heard, and friends send presents and congratulations.

In riding through the streets one day I dropped my fan—a cheap little thing I had purchased at Vancouver—and not worth stopping to recover. A week later I entered a small shop, and there sat the proprietor, fanning himself with the lost article. My initials were on it, and purely for mischief I pointed to it and said, "Ikura?" ("How much?") As he shook his head and clutched his treasure, a faint, inscrutable smile passed over his countenance. It was the ugliest and least desirable fan in his shop, and I left him in undisturbed possession of his souvenir. Later, I learned that the Japanese have a superstition that if a man find a fan lying in the road, he is likely in the future to become a member of some noble family. I rejoice to have so materially assisted in another's advancement.

One evidence of the piety and energy of old times is seen in the number and beauty of the temples built and kept in repair

Tokyo.

all over the kingdom, but we were greatly impressed by the apparent decay of religion. Their church festivals are holiday gatherings, their pilgrimages social outings. The Shintō is the true religion of Japan, and the rites prescribed by it are ancestor worship and filial piety. The worship is as ancient as the race. Their private devotions are limited to a "God-shelf" in every house, on which is a Shintō shrine, enclosing the memorial tablets of deceased relatives, and a Shintō mirror of steel, in which they are supposed to see their sins, as they do their distorted features. The great Buddhist temple of Asakusa is the most popular in Tōkyō, and there religion and pleasure mingle in delightful disorder. Several hundred years ago, a small figure of Kwannon, the goddess of mercy, was found in the river near by. It was declared to have dropped from the skies; it has since been preserved as a sacred relic, and can be seen to this day in the temple. No goddess has so many worshippers as she, or was ever adored with more ardent devotion. The temple and grounds are the great holiday resort of the middle and lower classes; the neighborhood is well supplied with theatres and tea-houses; and the broad paved avenue that leads to the entrance is lined with booths, where photographic views, all manner of ingenious toys, gewgaws, sweetmeats, and food are sold. I was urged to try a small brown rice-cake, an innocent-looking affair, and shall never forget how horrible it was; I had tasted some awful mixtures in the past month, but nothing that could compare with that morsel fried in fish-oil.

As we walked along, throngs of children with queer eyes

In Bamboo Lands.

and untidy noses clustered around us and pulled our skirts. This we endured with a good grace for a while, until, weary, we brought it to an end. A Japanese friend had kindly provided us with a phrase to use when annoyed in this way, and we tried it with telling effect. They shrank away with horror depicted on their faces, but, as I know neither the meaning of it nor how to spell it, I will not attempt to write it. We had a second experience at Kyōtō with the same satisfactory result.

The natives of the Orient are well known for their superstition, and the shops in which charm-bags are sold are numberless. A charm usually has the name of some god upon it, or a quotation from Buddhist scripture. The custom of wearing an amulet is universal; young children wear them tied about the waist, adults conceal them in the girdle, and the aged, anxious to stand well with the gods, wear any number of them. There is a superstitious impression that they have occult power to ward off evil, and to drop one is accounted unlucky and foretells speedy death. While in the towns superstition is to some extent dying out, it still holds undivided sway in isolated provinces, where the natives have not been brought into contact with Europeans. Farther on are booths filled with idols of brass and wood, incense-burners, and other devotional articles.

We came upon a small shrine of Jizō and a prayer wheel— the symbol of faith. The prayers are not written as in India; the suppliant merely turns the wheel, with the simple request that Jizō will let his sins pass by unnoticed, that he may not be punished for them in a future state. The idea is essentially

Tokyo.

this; that our misfortunes are the result of sins committed in a past existence; that acts and thoughts outlive a man's life and are projected beyond to shape other lives yet unborn; that which we are is the consequence of that which we have been. The entrance gate is a high wooden structure painted red, with

DAIBUTSU, ASAKASA.

hideous figures of the Ni-ō (Two Kings) on either side, protected by wire netting. The network was spotted with bits of chewed paper, thrown by persons who believe that if they stick the prayers written on them will be granted. The gate was hung with exaggerated straw sandals, placed there by

In Bamboo Lands.

coolies anxious to excel in walking. The main temple, of wood painted a dark red, is covered by an enormous sweeping roof, inseparable from structures of this class. Between the huge circular columns of the portico, paper lanterns, ten feet long, dangled from the eaves. The custom of not wearing shoes in the temple is not observed here; and as the floor was exceedingly dirty, we were correspondingly thankful. The decorations of the interior are unique. Among a confused mass of lanterns covered with yellow dragons and banners with strange devices, that hung from the cross-beams, we saw gaudily framed prints of steamship companies and flocks of pigeons that find unmolested homes among the handsome wood-carvings of the ceiling. Clouds of incense rise continually from a massive bronze burner near the entrance. A seated image of Bin-zuru, a Buddhist saint who has a special reputation as a healer, is worn smooth and glossy by constant friction. Believers rub the affected part against a like portion of the god, seemingly with more danger of contracting than of curing disease. Priests with heads completely shaved, and wearing very loose garments with wide sleeves, sit on the floor in front of the shrines and relics. The chancel is separated from the nave by a coarse wire frame; but an offering to the priest admitted us. The high altar, draped with fine old embroidery, supported the beautiful gilded shrine that contains the historic image of Kwannon. Around it are smaller figures, gilded and painted, candlesticks, bells, idols, incense vases of bronze, and other trappings of Buddhist worship. The greatest noise and confusion prevailed, and we hastened

Tokyo.

out after casting a few sen into the big wooden treasury box and purchasing little packets of sweet-smelling sticks to burn in honor of the goddess. An image of Jizō, the especial patron of children and all who are in trouble, occupies a building in the rear. Ranged in line about him were countless small stone figures of dead little ones placed there by afflicted parents. It was really a very pathetic sight. An innumerable number of stone images of this popular deity are to be met on the highways throughout the land.

The building that contains the "Revolving Library" also deserves notice. On the eaves are rich carvings of lions, and the interior is still more beautifully decorated. The shrine of gorgeous red lacquer contains a complete collection of Buddhist scriptures. As an ordinary lifetime is too short to enable an individual to read all these books, it is arranged that the same degree of merit may be obtained, and the reward will be long life and prosperity, if he "will cause the library to revolve three times on its axis." It was an opportunity not to be neglected—we paid the fee, and, assisted by willing hands, accomplished the feat.

The temple grounds are now a public park, where amusements of all kinds flourish. One sees on every side shooting-alleys, acrobats, wrestlers, jugglers, theatres, and sellers of toys and sweets—all doing a thriving business. In the midst of this medley was a troop of monkeys that snatched ravenously at the food tendered them, and then expressed their gratitude by bowing to the ground in true Japanese fashion.

In Bamboo Lands.

We saw a collection of strange plants and curious birds on exhibition in a native house; also a crude panorama of our Civil War. The most extraordinary sight of all was the orderly, good-natured crowd hobbling along with great clatter of wooden sandals, bent on having a good time. They still eye foreigners with some curiosity, but not unpleasantly; and

THE BELL TEMPLE AT ASAKASA.

courtesy and good order reigned where individuals brushed against each other at every turn. The Japanese are the most interesting people it has been my good fortune to be among. This gathering-place has frequently been compared to an

Tokyo.

English county fair; but it seems to me its counterpart cannot be found on this planet.

Our remaining weeks in Japan were getting few, and we had still much to see. Our stay in Tōkyō had been entirely satisfactory, our relations with our landlady had been eminently pleasant, but we felt impelled to leave for Kyōtō, whither an irresistible curiosity was drawing us. We sorrowfully packed our traps and said, not good-by, but *au revoir*, and departed, after a droll and exciting adventure. I cannot resist the temptation of putting it down. The Japanese officials reserve to themselves the right of regulating the affairs of tourists, and sometimes avail themselves of it. Our party of three arrived at the station on our way to Yokohama, one lady remaining without while we two went in to purchase the tickets. My companion laid down the money for two and I the price of one. The clerk handed us two tickets, took pay for two, and refused to sell a third. He had his own system of logic; he saw but two persons and declined to be a party to such extravagance. Entreaty did not melt his heart; he was inexorable. We used all the Japanese words we knew and some that were not Japanese, but all in vain—he merely shook his head with an Oriental composure that nearly drove us frantic. As the train was about to start I prevailed upon my friend to take the tickets and go on board, while I persisted in my task. As he could neither understand nor I explain, the case was serious. Fortunately, at the very last moment an official less capricious appeared, who was willing to do me the favor of allowing me to squander my own if I wished to.

In Bamboo Lands.

I expressed my boundless gratitude in one word, "Arigato," ("Thank you"), grasped my ticket, rushed through the turnstile, dashed down the platform as the whistle for departure sounded, leaped into a carriage, and the guard banged the door.

CHAPTER V.

THE TOKAIDO.

THE most celebrated highway in Japan is the old Tōkaidō, bordered on either side with ancient cryptomerias, and along which the daimyōs with princely magnificence used to travel on their way to the Shōgun's court at Tōkyō.

In its palmy days what scenes it must have presented? Norimons (palanquins of the nobles), kagos (basket conveyances for the middle class), packhorses carrying merchandise, and crowds of men, women, and children on foot travelling slowly and stopping frequently at tea-houses for rest and refreshment. When the trains of two princes—either on horseback or carried in chairs—met, it was etiquette for the one of lower degree to alight and withdraw with his train to the side of the road until the other had passed, and woe betide him if he failed to submit to his superior. Even down to the present time foreigners ignorant of the practice of the country occasionally have unpleasant encounters with conservative members of this haughty class, who cling rigidly to the customs of "Old Japan," and are compelled by them to dismount and give the road. One day, in riding along the highway near Numazu, we espied one of the old *régime* approaching; and, rather than subject American citizens to a humiliating or-

In Bamboo Lands.

deal, we fled up the steps to a shrine and waited for his excellency to pass by.

Numerous trains of two-sworded men in feudal war-costume were a striking feature of this road in the good old times. They crowded the towns, too—for a nobleman never appeared in public without armed defenders; and two-sworded men were legion. They passed out of existence with feudalism in 1868, and their beautiful swords have degenerated into curios. The Japanese swords, which rival the famous products of Damascus and Toledo, that could "be bent into a circle," are wrought by armorers quite as famous. They are "made of soft, elastic, magnetic iron, combined with hard steel," and so well tempered as to cut through a copper coin without turning the edge. The ancient sword for dispatching one's enemies is three feet long, has two edges, and is wielded with both hands. The short sword, for dispatching one's self, is less than ten inches in length. The sword-sellers are numerous, and in their shops one may see many an ancient blade, exquisitely finished, that has been tried and tested in the wars of feudal times. The scabbards, too, richly inlaid with silver on the bronze, bear testimony to the cunning of the workmen who wrought the weapon.

The Tōkaidō skirts the coast along a strip of flat country lying between the hills and the sea. From Yokohama we travelled to Kyōtō in the west by the Tōkaidō railway, breaking the journey at several points of interest. At the small station of Kōzu, we left the train, devoting a half-hour to the beach and its fine sea-views before taking the tram-car to

ON THE ROAD TO MIYANOSHITA.

The Tokaido.

Yumoto, where we hired kurumas and two men each to carry us to Miyanoshita, a resort in the mountains well known by reputation for its scenery of peculiar richness and variety, its natural warm baths, and the charming excursions in the vi-

DOGASHIMA, NEAR MIYANOSHITA.

cinity. We passed through picturesque hamlets embedded in foliage, and wound up among the gently swelling hills with their tiny waterfalls and crystal rivulets trickling down the sides. Nature has been very lavish in these wilds, and it was the loveliest short ride I enjoyed in Japan.

In Bamboo Lands.

We took up our quarters at the Fujita Hotel—an excellent one in foreign style. The walks were exhilarating, and though we had kagos with us—as the paths in many places are rough and precipitous—we seldom rode, and the coolies had a sinecure. Day after day of glorious sunshine we spent in that dreamy, delicious air, wandering through valleys watered by mountain streams, forcing our way through tangled thickets and beds of matted fern, visiting temples and shrines without number, stopping in quaint little villages to rest and to sip tea, and climbing heights for views of Fujiyama and other lofty peaks. The sweet air was fragrant with the spicy odors of the pine-trees; azaleas, scrub-bamboo, dense clumps of ferns and flowers in profusion surrounded us, and vines tangled the branches overhead. The evenings on the veranda were not less delightful. We left there reluctantly, sending our baggage on by packhorse, while we rambled over the hills to Hakone, five miles distant. The weather was lovely; the varied vegetation was glorious in autumn gold and copper; and although we lingered to gather fronds of fern, scarlet lilies, and relics of departing summer, our destination was reached in less than three hours.

Hakone, at the head of a lake of the same name, is one thousand feet higher than Miyanoshita, its rival, as a summer resort. The hotel overlooks this pretty sheet of water five miles long, and so attractive that we handed the landlord our passports to be inspected at leisure, hastened to the shore, engaged a boat, and soon were floating along its rippling surface. The lake is encircled by mountains that slope to the water's

FUJIYAMA.

The Tokaido.

edge, and small farms and hamlets fringe the shore; but everything is totally eclipsed by the sublime view of Fujiyama peering down from the clouds—a picture that would make the reputation of any artist that could transfer it to canvas. Recent snows had covered the mountain with a pure white mantle dazzling to the eyes in the autumn sunshine, and no description which I could give would approach the reality. Fujiyama is singularly impressive, and like Mauna Loa, Kinchinjanga, and Shasta, commands a half unwilling reverence.

The minor attractions of Hakone are the temple of Gongen shaded by old pines, the Emperor's summer palace, two iron rice boilers—relics of the twelfth century—and excursions in every direction, the most beautiful of which is that across the Ten Province Pass to Atami on Odawara Bay. The autumn was fine, and the day spent there brought instinctively to mind the remembrance of lovely Alp-sheltered Nice, its orange groves, and the blue Mediterranean flare.

Shimoda, a little to the south, was first visited by Commodore Perry in 1854, and there four United States marines are buried. Our first envoy, Townsend Harris, was formally installed in the little town in 1856 and resided there for years until Yokohama was substituted as an open port.

We rode fifteen miles by kuruma along the Tōkaidō to the station of Numazu. It was on that day we happened upon the nobleman and gave him the road, and met two-wheeled carts made of rough timber and drawn by bullocks that gave us the road. These wagons, when loaded with newly cut bamboo, were picturesque in the extreme. They have no

In Bamboo Lands.

springs; I tried one for a short distance, and it nearly jolted the life out of me.

A feature of Japanese journeys by rail is the ever-present teapot. At every important station, pots of freshly made tea are brought into the car, whose contents you are expected to buy and consume, to be ready for the next instalment. We had no desire to emulate the Japanese in tea-drinking; but on that intolerably hot and dusty ride it was strangely refreshing.

The views from the carriage windows were magnificent; the mountains rose in majesty to the right—the sea spread out for miles to the left. At Mio-no-Matsubara is laid the scene of the "Robe of Feathers," a charming tale from Japanese folklore. Many years ago a fisherman, landing on the beach, found hanging to a tree a robe of feathers. He was about to carry it away, when a beautiful fairy with golden tresses and eyes like the sky appeared and claimed it as her own. The fisherman at first declined to give up his costly treasure; but without it she could not return to the moon, where she was an attendant of the "thirty monarchs" who rule that orb. After tears and entreaty on her part, he finally consented—on condition that she should dance for him one of the dances of the immortals. Decked in her light, airy garment, she danced on the sunlit beach, while ethereal notes and elysian sweets perfumed the air. Then the breezes caught her wings and she mounted upward, like a spirit "who from heaven hath flown," and was lost to sight.

We passed through Shizuoka, where the ex-Shōgun Keiki, the last representative of that "peculiar system" of govern-

THE FISHING INDUSTRY

The Tokaido.

ment founded by Yoritomo in 1192, lives in retirement as a private gentleman. It would have been a satisfaction to have met him, but his seclusion is inviolable.

The great bridge that spans the Kanaya River is an iron structure fully a mile in length. As our train passed over we saw nothing but sky and a waste of sand and boulders, and wondered what all the fuss was about. When half-way across we discovered a narrow, neglected-looking stream flowing quietly between desert banks. But this river has a habit of getting out of its little bed. The greater portion of the island is covered by mountains; and, owing to the narrowness of the land, most Japanese streams are torrents rather than rivers. When the snow melts in the mountains or after thunderstorms, by which the country is often visited, these streams bring down enormous volumes of water, and become raging floods that crowd their way to the sea, sweeping away bridges and dikes and overflowing the plains.

I once knew a fisherman on the River St. Lawrence who would lie idly in his boat, with a bell attached to his rod, and wait for the fish to notify him when caught. He told me that the device was original—and undoubtedly it was; but on the lagoon at Hamamatsu the fishermen have for ages fastened bells on their nets to indicate the presence of fish, showing that in widely distant lands similar conditions lead to similar inventions and habits.

We became so interested in watching our favorite pastime that we missed our train and were forced to spend the night at a native hotel. No one who has ever stayed at a Japanese

In Bamboo Lands.

inn is likely to forget the experience—they are all alike and all equally uncomfortable; but a lovely sail on the lagoon that evening was compensation for all hardship.

A rice-producing province extends for a hundred miles along the coast. The fields cover the lowlands and run up the terraced hillsides among clumps of bamboo and dark masses of forest. The whole country was yellow with ripening grain about to be harvested, and myriads of birds or "white waders" flew from field to field or stalked about in the mire. The infinite network of rice-field paths—low grass-tufted ridges—divides the spaces into all sizes and shapes, a quarter of an acre being the ordinary size. The water for irrigating the "paddy fields," as they are called, is raised into ditches by means of a roughly constructed portable paddle-wheel turned by treading, and is then skilfully led on from field to field. The plough, a long-toothed instrument that turns up a three-foot furrow, is drawn by a horse that is guided by a rod of bamboo attached to his nose. The seed is soaked until nearly ready to sprout, and then sown thickly in small fields or nurseries that are flooded each night and drawn off during the day. When the plants are three inches high they are taken up in tufts of four, and transplanted at distances of a foot apart, where they grow in water until ready to harvest, when the fields are drained off.

Rice culture must be a very disagreeable occupation, as the weeding is done by people wading knee-deep in mud and water. Women perform much of the outdoor work, and we noticed them toiling in the rice-swamps with infants strapped

RICE FIELDS.

The Tokaido.

to their backs, who were being shaken about unmercifully and who slept through it all.

It is a mistaken idea that rice is the staple article of food in Japan. It is cultivated very generally by the peasants and sold to the townspeople; for, with the former, rice is a luxury to be used only on holidays or in case of sickness. Millet, a little barley or wheat, dried fish, and seaweed constitute the principal articles of diet, supplemented by the pestilential daikon. How they can eat the latter is a mystery still unsolved. An acre of land yields about forty bushels of rice, and a nobleman's wealth is estimated by the number of kokus (five bushels) his estates produce. Prosperity is reckoned by the rice crop, and there are frequently serious failures.

We reached Nagoya that evening and found a public house recommended as "foreign"—a building of Japanese architecture enclosed by a wooden fence that reached to the second story. The exterior was unattractive; but, admitted past the gate, we rode into a neat courtyard with a garden in the rear. The hotel was not barbarian enough to tolerate boots; and, at the top of the steep staircase, we stood in stocking feet while the landlord examined the passports—the natives show so little regard for the hosiery and health of tourists. As the dividing walls did not reach the ceiling, the whole house intercommunicated; the slightest noise could be heard to the remotest corner, and attendants must be summoned not by ringing a bell—there were none—but by clapping the hands. The dining-room overlooked the garden, and was supplied with a row of tables, each of which could be enclosed in a separate

In Bamboo Lands.

room by drawing the sliding screens. This was done with a great rattle the instant a second party entered. No table d'hôte or bill of fare greeted us—guests were expected to order their own meals, after untold trials in finding out the contents of the larder. The limited variety of food, however, was well cooked, and we rang the changes on chickens, ham, eggs, toast, and the indispensable tea.

Before retiring we strolled through the principal thoroughfare thronged with people enjoying the moonlight. It was a warm evening; the moon was full, and not a cloud obscured her light or that of the countless stars which bore her company. The shops were opened wide for business and the sidewalks lined with booths for refreshments, where the cooking was going on in full sight and greasy odors filled the air. The paper lantern shops were conspicuous. The usual shape of the article is oblong; they are of all sizes, frequently twelve feet in length, and ornamented with every color and design that fancy can suggest. No festival is complete without them. We visited a bazaar where everything engaged the attention, but the heat and the crowd drove us out, and we returned to the hotel to make plans for the morrow and to dispatch our passports and "letters" to the prefectural office for a permit to visit the "Castle." European beds and bedclothes were a luxury after a night among the coverlets and centipedes; but mosquitoes were too numerous for our entire comfort. Those little pests here have the same accomplishments as musicians and leeches that they possess in other climes. They sang sprightly war-songs during their nimble repast, and the next

SIFTING RICE.

The Tokaido.

morning I discovered that the tastefully arranged drapery of my couch was a netting.

There was some delay in getting our permit, as the premises were closed for repairs, made necessary by the terrible earthquake of 1891.

The historic castle of Nagoya was an important stronghold during the time Japan was a feudal empire. Erected in 1610 as a residence for the son of Ieyasu, it has in later years been turned over to the military department, and the great space between the inner and outer moat is used for barracks and parade-grounds. We rode across the enclosure, where ten thousand troops were encamped. Could anything be more inconsistent than a regiment in European uniform executing European manœuvres before a shrine? The talisman was the Car of Hachiman, worshipped as the god of war. This was a platform covered by a canopy that held numbers of colossal swords and a great mirror—an emblem of Shintōism. (It is an important fact that modern German tactics and an education in the exact sciences do not remove the belief in omens, charms, and signs from the minds of these people. The proof can be found in this great castle of Nagoya, where the upper story is filled with small wooden slabs that are furnished by the priests to protect it against fire and other perils.) The place presented a most warlike appearance, and we asked in vain what meant all this preparation—what campaign they were meditating—with whom they were going to war—questions which have since been answered. The little country which has suddenly become so formidable felt that it must tell its greatness.

In Bamboo Lands.

It is not surprising the Japanese make efficient soldiers when it is remembered that they are a race of warriors bred to arms; their religion teaches them to place no value on life, and their emperor commands them to die by their own swords rather than fall into the enemy's hands. The soldier's duty is to fight, and to fight to the death, giving and taking no quarter. It is the old Samurai spirit which still lives on. Japan has a standing army of three hundred thousand men. The policy of the government is to learn of Europeans and then dispense with their services, and there is now not a single foreigner connected with the army or navy in any capacity whatever. The Japanese have a special talent for learning Western methods and incredible courage in using their knowledge, and the wisest cannot foresee to what degree it will develop.

We left the great Hachiman and his still greater retinue at their exercises and crossed the bridge over the inner moat, dry and the home of tame deer, to the "apartments," which, with the castle, are preserved as show-places. The rooms are denuded of mats, but the alcoves and panels are richly decorated with paintings of flowers and birds by artists of the famous Kano school. In one of the first rooms are some sketches of cherry-blossoms and pheasants; in another scenes from daily life are depicted; and the finest of all—that reserved for the Shōgun—has gorgeous paintings of ideal Chinese scenery.

The castle, or "keep," is a stone pagoda of five stories; from the upper platform, reached by wooden stairs, the view is far-reaching. The roof is surmounted by two golden dol-

GOLDEN DOLPHIN.

The Tokaido.

phins, eight feet high and valued at one hundred and eighty thousand dollars. They can be seen as glittering points from every part of the city. The one sent to the Vienna exposition of 1873 was shipwrecked, but finally recovered and placed in its former position. The exterior of the castle was marred by scaffolding and the interior blocked by workmen engaged in its restoration, but, notwithstanding, our visit was most satisfactory.

By a magnificent two-storied gateway we entered the great courtyard, in the centre of which rises the temple of Higashi Hongwanji. A fine colonnade surrounds the exterior. The spacious interior is divided into compartments—the outer for observers, the centre for the congregation, and the inner for the altar, on which stands the handsome gilt shrine, containing an image of Amida, a powerful deity who dwells in the West. The walls and ceiling are very rich in ornamentation and each detail is a work of art. A stone with the imprint of Buddha's huge feet was noticed; but, as his height is said to have been sixteen feet, they are not out of proportion, as is not that tooth of his in the temple in Kandy.

In a certain gallery we saw the Go Hyaku Rakan, five hundred images of Buddha's chief followers. They are two feet in height, painted in bright colors, and no two are alike. On their faces are depicted every emotion, from grave to gay; and their shapes and attitudes express every gradation, from the sublime to the ridiculous. The place gives you the impression of a wilderness of diminutive howling dervishes. Tradition states that by careful search you can find among

In Bamboo Lands.

them the image of your own father; but even with the new philosophy of evolution in mind, it would shock one to recognize an ancestor in that hideous group. On entering one finds himself under a singular illusion: the apostles' faces are turned toward the observer and the eyes seem to say: "Do you recognize me?" We tarried not to discover, but hastened away from the rare good things so lavishly provided for our entertainment.

The potteries and the shops in which rare cloisonné enamels are made are numerous and attractive, and in them we saw specimens that were as fine as Japan produced in the seventeenth and eighteenth centuries—its golden age of art.

At noon the next day we were in Gifu, which suffered so terribly by the memorable earthquake of 1891, as did the entire coast as far as Nagoya. It was estimated that in Gifu alone ten thousand people lost their lives and that twenty thousand more were rendered homeless and destitute. Our English-speaking guide gave us a vivid description of the scenes of horror during the cataclysm: the earth burst open in great fissures, and the frail houses of bamboo were crushed by the heavy tiled roofs before the inhabitants had time to escape. When we reached the scene the ruined homes still lay in hopeless confusion, sad witnesses of its violence; and the unfortunate citizens were as actively engaged in rebuilding as if they never expected a recurrence of the disaster. The earthquake is no stranger to the dwellers in that part of the world. Unfortunately Japan is specially subject to convulsions of nature, and it is the one thing that mars the enjoyment of a stay

GIFU IN RUINS.

The Tokaido.

there. The suffocating stillness of the atmosphere—the dull, rumbling roar—the very ground undulating beneath one's feet—are enough to disturb the mental equilibrium of a stoic. One can endure the slight shocks with tolerable composure, but I have passed through several in different parts of the world that have made me think the end of all things had come. A traveller in Japan who has any curiosity to feel an earthquake can be sure of having it gratified at any moment, and may be thankful if he escapes without an accident. The natives have a superstition that they are caused by the throes of a great subterranean fish; but, whatever be the cause, they are not companionable. Geologists believe that much of Japan has been elevated above the ocean by seismic disturbances, and the country has paid dearly for additional territory by the sacrifice of hundreds of thousands of lives. We went to Gifu to view the ruins and remained to see the strange method of fishing with cormorants on the River Nagara. We secured boats and followed the procession.

"First catch your cormorant. . . . This the people do by placing wooden images of the birds in spots frequented by them, and covering the surrounding branches and twigs with birdlime, on settling upon which they stick fast. After having in this manner caught one cormorant, they place it among the bushes instead of the image, and thus catch more. . . . The fishermen take such care of the birds that they provide them with mosquito nets during the summer in order to minister to their comfort. Cormorant-fishing always takes place at night and by torchlight." A letter written by Major-General Pal-

In Bamboo Lands.

mer and published in the London *Times* thus describes the method pursued:

"There are, to begin with, four men in each of the seven boats, one of whom, at the stern, has no duty but that of managing his craft. In the bow stands the master, distinguished by the peculiar hat of his rank, and handling no fewer than twelve trained birds with the surpassing skill and coolness that have earned for the sportsmen of Gifu their unrivalled pre-eminence. Amidships is another fisher, of the second grade, who handles four birds only. Between them is the fourth man, called kako, from the bamboo striking-instrument of that name, with which he makes the clatter necessary for keeping the birds up to their work; he also encourages them by shouts and cries, looks after spare apparatus, etc., and is ready to give aid if required. Each cormorant wears at the base of its neck a metal ring, drawn tight enough to prevent marketable fish from passing below it, but at the same time loose enough—for it is never removed—to admit the smaller prey, which serves as food. Round the body is a cord, having attached to it at the middle of the back a short strip of stiffish whalebone, by which the great awkward bird may be conveniently lowered into the water or lifted out when at work; and to this whalebone is looped a thin rein of spruce fibre twelve feet long, and so far wanting in pliancy as to minimize the chance of entanglement. When the fishing-ground is reached, the master lowers the twelve birds one by one into the stream and gathers their reins into his left hand, manipulating the latter thereafter with his right as occasion requires.

The Tōkaidō.

No. 2 does the same with his four birds; the kako starts in with his volleys of noise; and forthwith the cormorants set to at their work in the heartiest and jolliest way, diving and ducking with wonderful swiftness as the astonished fish come flocking toward the blaze of light. The master is now the busiest of men. He must handle his twelve strings so deftly that, let the birds dash hither and thither as they will, there shall be no impediment or fouling. He must have his eyes everywhere and his hands following his eyes. Specially must he watch for the moment when any of his flock is gorged, a fact generally made known by the bird itself, which then swims about in a foolish, helpless way, with its head and swollen neck erect. Thereupon the master, shortening in on that bird, lifts it aboard, forces its bill open with his left hand, which still holds the rest of the lines, squeezes out the fish with his right and starts the creature off on a fresh foray—all this with such admirable dexterity and quickness that the eleven birds still bustling about have scarce time to get things into a tangle, and in another moment the whole team is again perfectly in hand.

"As for the cormorants, they are trained when quite young, being caught in winter with birdlime on the coasts of the neighboring Owari Gulf at their first emigration southward from the summer haunts of the species on the northern seaboard of Japan. Once trained, they work well up to fifteen, often up to nineteen or twenty years of age; and, though their keep in winter bears hardly on the masters, they are very precious and profitable hunters during the five months' season

In Bamboo Lands.

and well deserve the great care that is lavished upon them. From four to eight good-sized fish, for example, is the fair result of a single excursion for one bird, which corresponds to an average of about one hundred and fifty fish per cormorant per hour, or about four hundred and fifty for the three hours occupied in drifting down the whole course. Every bird in a flock has and knows its number; and one of the funniest things about them is the quick-witted jealousy with which they invariably insist, by all that cormorant language and pantomimic protest can do, on due observance of the recognized rights belonging to their individual numbers. No. 1, or "Ichi," is the doyen of the corps, the senior in years as well as rank. His colleagues, according to their ages, come after him in numerical order. Ichi is the last to be put into the water and the first to be taken out, the first to be fed, and the last to enter the baskets in which, when work is over, the birds are carried from the boats to their domicile. Ichi, when aboard, has the post of honor at the eyes of the boat. He is a solemn, grizzled old fellow, with a pompous, *noli-me-tangere* air, that is almost worthy of a lord mayor. The rest have place after him, in succession of rank, alternately on either side of the gunwale. If, haply, the lawful order of precedence be at any time violated—if, for instance, No. 5 be put into the water before No. 6, or No. 4 be placed above No. 2, the rumpus that forthwith arises in that family is a sight to see and a sound to hear.

"But all this while we have been drifting down with the boats about us, to the lower end of the course, and are again

The Tōkaidō.

abreast of Gifu, where the whole squadron is beached. As each cormorant is taken out of the water the master can tell by its weight whether it has secured enough supper while engaged in the hunt; failing which, he makes the deficiency good by feeding it with the inferior fish of the catch. At length all are ranged in their due order, facing outward, on the gunwale of each boat. And the sight of that array of great ungainly seabirds—shaking themselves, flapping their wings, gawing, making their toilets, clearing their throats, looking about them with a stare of stupid solemnity, and now and then indulging in old-maidish tiffs with their neighbors—is quite the strangest of its little class I have ever seen, except perhaps the wonderful penguinry of the Falkland Islands, whereat a certain French philosopher is said to have even wept. Finally, the cormorants are sent off to bed"—we followed suit.

CHAPTER VI.

KYOTO.

Kyōtō is one of the most ancient cities in the kingdom and has been the capital of the Mikado for a period of one thousand years, ending in 1868.

Saikyō, its new name, little known to foreigners, has a vast collection of groves, gardens, temples, palaces, pagodas, shrines, and works of art, such as cannot be seen elsewhere in Japan. The city, which has greatly shrunken in modern times, lies on a plain encircled by broken ranges of mountains, densely wooded, and the whole country is clothed in luxuriant vegetation.

In order to fully appreciate and enjoy the show places of Kyōtō and all that in it is spread out for one's pleasure, one must be familiar with the history, the religion, and the art of Japan. The city is famed for its brocades and embroidery, its lacquered ware, cloisonné, porcelain, and weapons; it contains twenty-five hundred Shintō shrines and thirty-five hundred Buddhist temples; and every man who was great in the annals of his country has left his mark there.

Our train reached the railway station at night. The procession of twenty kurumas with passengers and baggage made a great clatter as we rode through the dark streets, two miles,

Kyoto.

to the hotel. No light appeared through chinks of sliding screens; not a voice, not a footstep was heard; not a living soul was to be seen, and up above—far above—shone the silent, eternal stars. We wondered what the awakened sleepers thought about us and how they expressed their displeasure under the circumstances.

The Yaami hotel—in foreign style but managed by Japanese—is situated on the hillside of Maruyama and overlooks the city and its environs. The house is peculiarly constructed, in three distinct parts, joined by open galleries, and the effect is pleasing. It has broad piazzas and comfortable steamer-chairs, and the views are well worth travelling to Japan for. The garden is charming; a brook tumbles over rockeries in tiny cascades, the pools are filled with goldfish, hedges outline the paths, and a soft carpet of grass covers the lawn. In the midst of all stand cherry and plum trees, dwarf pines, a gray and mossy stone shrine, and a temple lantern. Snails make their homes on the smooth rocks wet with constant spray, and we disposed of many a leisure moment in searching for left-handed specimens.

In this delightful abode we established ourselves for a stay of some weeks. Our large, well-furnished rooms opened on a veranda—all our own—that commanded a magnificent view toward the west; and there, in the late afternoon, we reclined in comfort to observe the sunset and watch the evening shadows wrap the mountains in their soft embrace. The displays were magnificent. Violet, green, orange, and gold streaked the sky into a perfect kaleidoscope of ever-changing colors

In Bamboo Lands.

fading slowly into the quiet grays of twilight; and far off, toward the horizon, distant ranges showed faintly in the glowing blue. We would indulge in fanciful reveries or talk on in the sweet autumn darkness until the stars twinkled out overhead and the soft tinkle of the samisen floated upward from the tea-houses on the avenue—hours that dwell in my mind as a blissful memory, and I look wistfully toward Maruyama, with a thousand tender associations.

There were so many good things to see in Kyōtō, we felt we should be up and about our sight-seeing. The guide-book suggested the Mikado's palace; but we must show proper respect to our hillside neighbor, and selected the temple of Chion-in for our first day's pleasure. This temple of the Jōdō sect of Buddhists is approached by a broad avenue lined with enormous old cherry-trees, whose blossoms have drawn worshipping crowds for three centuries. At the summit stands the great gateway, a large, two-storied structure eighty feet in height, which we entered Again we removed our shoes. Leaving them in charge of women who pick up a little "cash" by this means, we climbed a ladder to the upper room occupied by images of the gods. Buddha in meditation, with half-closed eyelids, is seated between two other deities and attended by sixteen life-sized figures of his disciples in fanciful costumes.

The glorious views from the outer gallery were worth the climb, but the descent was both perilous and ludicrous. Dangling between earth and heaven we laughed immoderately, while the Buddhas who sat in state above, and the women who

TEMPLE OF CHION-IN.

Kyoto.

held our boots below, looked on in evident disapproval of foreign levity. By two long flights of steps we reached the paved courtyard, in the centre of which stands the great temple, surmounted by an enormous roof. Legend states that ages ago an umbrella flew from the hands of a small boy and lodged under the eaves, and that Inari, the patron deity of this monastery, promptly declared both the boy and the article sacred. The former has disappeared, but the latter, tattered and faded, we discovered after persistent search. The shrine of Enkō Daishi, to whom the temple is dedicated, rests on a platform surmounted by four gilt pillars, before which stand great bunches of lotus-flowers and leaves of brass in bronze vases. A feature of the temple is the oval-shaped, scarlet-lacquered mokugyo (bells) disposed on the matting before the altar. The priests with shaven heads chant without ceasing, "*Namu myo ho renge kyo*," squatted before these bells, on which they pound to wake up the gods. The interior was very effective, and entirely unlike any other we had seen.

WAKING UP THE GODS.

We were shown through the palace of the Shōgun Iemitsu in the same grounds; the doors, sliding screens, and panels are exquisite. In this building are the famous whistling boards, which, as we stepped upon them, emitted low, un-

In Bamboo Lands.

earthly sounds. In the high woods near the palace is the belfry that contains the great bronze bell cast in 1633; it weighs seventy-four tons and is rung like the one at Nikkō. The grand old temple had laid its charm upon us, and we returned again and again to wander in and out among its shrines and groves and derive new pleasure from each visit.

By a lovely path through the woods we returned to our hotel and entered by a rear door. We found ourselves in the cooking-department, a large low room with floor of earth, and furnished with rows of small fireplaces and charcoal braziers, utensils of primitive make in fine bronze and iron, and an array of lacquered plates and trays. The room was neatness itself. As it was the hour for afternoon tea, a score of "boys" were busy in its preparation, and we hastened to our charming piazza and restful chairs to enjoy it. The suburb in which the hotel is situated is occupied by tea-houses, where seekers of pleasure resort for dining, drinking, music, and dancing. Primitive customs still prevail, but slightly altered by European innovations. At night lights twinkle from every little inn, and we could watch the guests and the geishas who are let out in groups to entertain natives at their feasts, and are considered such an important item that a dinner would be a complete failure without their services. It was a rare opportunity to see the people unseen by them. The first night I scarcely closed my eyes, the beating of Buddhist drums at Chion-in outrivalling the noise and discords of the tea-houses; it was too much, but we soon became accustomed to both and rather enjoyed the absurd combination.

Kyoto.

A large amount of the porcelain produced in Japan is made in the suburb of Awata, which gives its name to this well-known ware. We visited a number of these potteries. Alighting before a dingy wooden building, the door was quickly opened by a servitor who ushered us into a showroom whose cabinets were filled with beautiful porcelain, cloisonné, damascene, and lacquer. Each piece was a work of art in fineness of finish, subdued coloring, and delicate ornamentation. The Japanese are born with a love of beauty and instinctive good taste, as is evinced by all wares manufactured for their own use; but, as they have quickly discovered what sells best in Europe and America, they now produce great quantities of cheap articles loaded with coarse decoration for foreign trade. We were taken into the packing-room, which was crowded with specimens of the gaudy red and gold vases that one sees in every china store from London to San Francisco. The proprietor took occasion to remark, as he pointed to his wares, "Japanese no like." It was cruel.

We walked through the garden to the factory. The article is first moulded and dried by fire, then glazed and fired, then decorated and fired again. The whole process is to be seen, from the kneading of the clay to the painting and firing, all done by hand-labor and with the crudest of tools. The finest pieces, not intended for "savages," are often fired many times according to the perfection of finish desired. The best decorators inherit much of their skill from generations of artists. Ceramic art in Japan dates from the year 1600 A.D., and the celebrated artist Ninsei originated Awata faience in 1650.

In Bamboo Lands.

The first half of the present century was the golden age of Satsuma, and that which ranks as "old Satsuma" is not so very ancient after all.

Kyōtō is well named the "City of Temples," and it was well for us that it was also a city of shops, or but a confused memory of them would have remained; and after a morning spent in the former we usually finished the day in the latter. Our old infirmity had returned in full force and never abated while we were in the fascinating old town.

On our way to the Yasaka pagoda we walked up a stair-like street lined with shops stuffed to their utmost capacity with trifles in bronze, porcelain, and bamboo, both pretty and inexpensive, for whatever the Japanese fashion it is always artistic. In one of the houses that cluster about the pagoda there was a lot of little monkeys, that for a few sen we were allowed to feed. When gratified they salaamed with great ceremony, but if neglected they would scold until the offender was out of sight.

The five-storied pagoda was raised about the year 1600 on the site of a former one. Except for a few paintings of Buddhist deities that adorn its panels, the interior is plain and disappointing, but from the top one gets a bird's-eye view of the whole city of Kyōtō, with its mass of one-story houses shabby with time, and all around a plain of vivid green encircled by mountains. The steep temple roofs scattered about the town serve as landmarks.

The temple of the great Buddha has had an eventful history, having been repeatedly destroyed by fire and earthquake.

THE GREAT BELL.

Kyoto.

In 1662 a violent shock levelled both the building and its bronze image to the ground. The Shōgun Iemitsu, being in need of funds, caused the bronze to be fused into coins, some of which are in circulation at this day. They are distinguished by the character 大, and by good chance I secured two. The present image of wood consists of head and shoulders only, but is so huge it reaches from floor to ceiling of the lofty temple. The great gilded head is hollow and supported by a network of beams; the temple walls are hung with cheap paintings, and the whole effect is tawdry. The interest of the place centres in the enormous bronze bell, weighing sixty-three tons, that hangs in the courtyard—second in size only to that of Chion-in, the two being the largest bells in Japan. Our guide was eager to exhibit the *divertisse-*

ANCIENT COIN.

ment of the grounds—a venerable mound, beneath which are buried the noses and ears of Koreans slain in the wars of the sixteenth century and brought home by the soldiers as trophies, they being more easily transported than heads. He fairly danced with glee as he made an elaborate explanation.

The heights of Maruyama, covered with thick green tinted with orange shades, were so alluring we determined to make the ascent. It was a beautiful day, warm and bright; and our landlord offered for use as guide and interpreter a lad who proved to be a care rather than a comfort. We sauntered up among the tea-houses by shady paths that serve as public walks, scrambled up the dry bed of a torrent, and entered the

In Bamboo Lands.

forest. Suddenly we were confronted by a sign-board covered with Japanese characters and sketches of a terrifying nature, evidently a warning not to proceed. Amazed and perplexed, we appealed to our small guide. He was speechless. Here was a pretty business. In dense shade, with rocks and decaying logs about us, we searched carefully, and, finding nothing of a harmful nature, we decided it must be a caution against snakes. The motive was not sufficient, however. We had seen too many reptiles of that genus in Japan to be driven back, and, arming ourselves with staves, we proceeded on our way, stumbling bravely along and reaching the summit in a rather shaky condition. On the hilltop, shaded by clumps of oak, we sat on a grassy knoll to rest and enjoy the magnificent prospect, with eyes and ears on the alert for impending danger. The autumn day was drowsy, the wind was soft and balmy, the sun shone through the masses of foliage above, and our nook and how we had wandered there became almost lost to remembrance. Encountering nothing alarming and utterly mystified as to the meaning of that sign, we reached the hotel to exhaust ourselves in query as to what the terrors of the hill might be, and all to no avail. You may imagine the curiosity which tormented us. At the end of a week our peace of mind was restored by the timely call of an English gentleman connected with the college. We told him of our experience, at which he laughed heartily, and revealed to us the astonishing fact that it was a warning to the public "not to gather mushrooms" and the penalty. We had looked for a mountain and discovered a mouse! What living being would expect to

SAN-JU-SAN-GEN-DO.

Kyoto.

find plants of that species at that elevation and under such conditions? But the spirit of topsy-turvydom, directly opposed to our ideas, has affected even this lowly fungus.

Here are a few Japanese contrarieties. They practically begin building their houses at the top. The roof is first constructed and set on four poles; the carpenter cuts and planes toward, instead of from, himself; the best rooms are at the back of the house, and rooms are made to fit the mats instead of mats to fit the rooms. They have no chimneys to their houses, the smoke finding its way out at the doors and windows. They wear white instead of black for mourning. They carry their babes on their backs, not in their arms. Boats are drawn on the shore stern first, and horses are tied in the stall with their heads where we place their tails. A Japanese book ends where ours begins. Wine is used before dinner, not after, and sweets are served as a first course. They politely remove their shoes as we do our hats, and when a man is insulted, instead of killing his enemy, he kills himself.

We took kurumas to San-jū-san-gen-dō, a temple that ranks next after Nikkō and Shiba in interest. Founded in 1132, it was rebuilt in 1266 by the Emperor Kameyama, who placed in it one thousand images of the thousand-handed Kwannon, the goddess of mercy. The exterior is unattractive, but upon entering there are few sights more imposing as the eye glances over the confused mass of glittering deities. In the centre of the great hall, three hundred and eighty-nine feet in length, the huge figure of Kwannon is seen, seated on an enormous lotus-flower of bronze, and ranged about her are twenty-eight

In Bamboo Lands.

of her followers. The altar is draped with damask and littered with many idols and shining objects that suggest Buddhism. On either side of the throne are rows of images of Kwannon, five feet in height, cut from solid blocks of wood and heavily gilded, rising tier behind tier; and on the halo, hands, and forehead of each figure are thirty-three smaller ones. Although these images represent the same deity, and the similarity is great, no two are exactly alike. We noticed a few natives prostrating themselves before these objects of worship, apparently engaged in prayer, with one eye directed toward the gods and the other toward us. The gallery in the rear was formerly used by archers, and it was a test of skill to shoot the arrows from one end and to fix them firmly in the opposite wall. We saw myriads of these little weapons sticking in the woodwork. The following description we obtained from a priest. I copy it *verbatim:*

THE ABRIDGEMENT OF SANJIŪ-SANGENDŌ IN KYŌTŌ, JAPAN.

This famous temple was built 730 years ago, in 1160 A.D. (1820 in the Japanese era, *i.e.* first years of Yeireki epoch). In that time our 77th emperor, Goshirakawa had been often afflicted by heavy headache. After every medical ait was tried in vain, His majesty being pious in Buddha ordered to build this temple, with thousand statues of Senju-Kwannon (the Buddha of Charity having thousandhands) in it, to pray for the restoration of sickness. The height of these idols is just equal to that of the Emperor himself, and other twenty-

Kyoto.

eight idols which are placed upon the steps of both sides in the front of temple are the guards for Kwannon with the sames, Kongo-Mishana-buddha, Kendatsu-ba-buddha, etc. The length of this temple is sixty-seven ken (one ken being about six feet) and the depth is nine ken. The name of Sanjiū-Sangendō, which implies 'the temple of thirty-three ken,' comes from that Kwannon vowed himself to solve us from the human misery by manifesting himself as thirty-three different bodies. It was about 300 years ago, in the time of our great Shōgun Toyotomi, that the famous matter of archery, which is to shoot bow through the verandah in the back of temple, took place. Hinceforce many warriors visited here to pray for their military fortunes, and especially these were flourishing about 180 years ago, during Kyōho epoch.   Sanjiū-Sangendō in Kyōtō, Japan."

A characteristic cemetery is that of Nishi Ōtani, the burial place of members of the Shinran Shōnin sect. The small temple is a handsome structure, and in the rear is an office containing the ashes of members from all parts of the country. The Kyōtō members are buried in the grounds, which are extensive, neatly kept, and crowded with square upright stones with inscriptions. Some of the monuments are very expensive and hung with chimes of bells that tinkle in the wind. The overcrowded effect is due to the custom of interring in a sitting posture in coffins but four feet high. Vines, rose-bushes, and bamboo grow wherever there is a spot of ground to cling to, and tall cryptomerias give character to the

In Bamboo Lands.

whole. A stone bridge, Megane-bashi (so named from its resemblance to a pair of spectacles) spans the lotus pond, which in summer is full of blossoms.

Cremation was introduced from China by the Buddhists,

NISHI ŌTANI.

and is extensively practised in Japan. The process of reducing to ashes is similar to ours. On one occasion we saw a native funeral procession on its way to the temple headed by a number of priests with shaven heads and cassocks of bright-colored damask, one of whom bore an oblong tablet inscribed with the "dead name" of the deceased, for good Buddhists re-

Kyoto.

ceive a new name after death, to be known by in the next world; then came attendants carrying twenty-four huge bouquets, six feet high, of chrysanthemums, and after them the hearse (a basket chair similar to those used at seaside resorts)

MEGANE-BASHI.

containing the covered remains, and borne by four men There were no hired mourners, but a long train of relatives and friends followed. It was an honorable and dignified funeral, quite unlike the unpleasing melancholy institution endured in America. In the temple, the burning of incense, the ringing of bells, and prayers intoned by the priests in a solemn,

In Bamboo Lands.

reverential manner formed the simple service. The death of a parent is the greatest misfortune that can befall a son, and the burial is a most important ceremony. For this duty he resigns all employment, attends to the many funeral rites ordained by custom, and mourns for thirteen months, wearing white garments during that period, and abstaining from animal food and sake for fifty days. When the prescribed details are respected the ceremonies before and after burial are very elaborate. Filial honor and obedience are leading virtues among the Japanese.

Marriage is a contract legalized by registration in the office of the head man of the town, termed kōcho. The usual age for a man is twenty years; for a woman sixteen. A lover fixes a sprig of lespedeza to the house of the lady's parents, and if that be neglected so is he; but if the maiden blackens her teeth he is accepted, subject to the approval of her parents. Marriages, however, are usually arranged by the families of the bride and bridegroom without reference to their feelings. And then begins a general interchange of presents, often so lavishly given as to cripple for a time the resources of the donors. This corresponds to betrothal. An engagement ring is unknown. A piece of rich silk for a sash takes its place. The furniture and trousseau of the bride are dispatched to the house of her husband's parents; and, after her arrival, the characteristic marriage feast is celebrated—there is no religious element in it—and is of the nature of a dinner party. The essential features are the changing of garments and the elaborate ceremony of sake-drinking. The registration is then

KURODANI

Kyoto.

made and the bride is formally adopted into her husband's family. A newly married pair invariably reside with the parents of the groom.

The life of a young girl, or mousme as she is called, is as careless and happy as the life of a European, but marriage is a stern reality. She then becomes subject to the tyranny of her mother-in-law and the caprice of her husband, and accepts her fate as a matter of course. The charge that "a man shall leave father and mother and cleave unto his wife" is reversed in Japan. Another case of topsy-turvydom. They insist that the wife shall leave father and mother and cleave to her husband and to all his relatives. There are seven reasons for divorce, which is easy and not rare, but the pith of the matter is that a man may send away his wife whenever he gets tired of her. "But her rights as against him are less extensive." This digression disposes of two important ceremonies.

The moral character of the Japanese—beg pardon, Dai Nippon; I was about to say something unpleasant of you.

A bridle-path runs from Nishi Ōtani through a grove of bamboo to the grounds of Kiyomizu-dera. A feeling of surprise and wonder attends the first view of this lovely foliage. Except in the Northern Island, it grows everywhere in Japan, softening and beautifying its fair landscape. Of its many species one variety in particular, whose lovely tips resemble magnificent ostrich-plumes, I grew to love and look for. Bamboo is the favorite hedge and wind-break along the highways. At one season the young and tender shoots are sought after as a great delicacy, and the wood, which is strong and

In Bamboo Lands.

pliable, enters into the construction of temples, houses, bridges, carriages, furniture, musical instruments, cooking-utensils, fans, hats, umbrellas, shoes, and almost every ornamental and useful article imaginable. The people are indebted to bamboo for a formidable list of gifts, so formidable it would be simpler to enumerate the exceptions.

The plants, fifty feet in height, then had attained their growth. The graceful feathery tips of light green drooped high overhead, and a wild tangle of ferns, mosses, bamboo-grass, and little stunted shrubs covered the embankments. It was a spot of rare beauty. The day was perfect. We could have lingered there the entire afternoon, and we made a point of including it thereafter in many of our daily walks.

Kiyomizu-dera, a temple so ancient its origin is lost in fable, was reached only too soon. The great two-story gateway was infested with fakirs and menders of old clothes, and we turned aside to a smaller gate that opened into the great courtyard, containing a pagoda and a number of shrines. An effective stone colonnade leads to the main temple, dedicated to the eleven-faced, thousand-handed Kwannon, who holds in her hands a number of Buddhist emblems, "such as the lotus-flower, the wheel of the law, the sun and moon, a skull, a pagoda, and an axe, this last serving to typify the cutting off of all worldly cares." Her image is contained in a shrine to be opened but once in thirty-three years. We were a decade or two behind time, but the powerful yen, like "the mighty dollar," opened it just the same. The building is large and erected on piles over a deep gorge. The gallery in front has

A WEDDING CEREMONY.

Kyoto.

a flooring of rough timber and is used as a dancing-stage. It was formerly a favorite resort of suicides, who threw themselves over to certain destruction on the rocks below. Recently a high railing has been built that has put a stop to the practice. These victims, inextricably entangled in love's net, usually die in pairs after solemnly pledging themselves to each other before a shrine.

The superstitions connected with love are endless, and occasionally a disappointment will drive a hopeless maiden to revenge. Having made a figure of straw which represents the disloyal lover, she repairs "at the hour of the ox," two in the morning, to a shrine in the wood and fastens the effigy to the sacred tree, asking the gods as she does so to impute the desecration to her lover and to avenge his perfidy. Several visits of this kind are supposed to have the desired effect. The lover gradually droops and dies—a sacrifice to love and grief, unique result of the exploits of that eccentric divinity whose antics are "as cruel as the grave." We left the grounds by the grand entrance and descended the long flights of steps, at the foot of which our kurumas awaited us.

This locality has been dubbed "teapot hill," from the numerous shops for the sale of these articles in every shape and pattern. The true Japanese teapot has a hollow handle placed at right angles, with a short, straight spout. An endless variety of sake bottles and cups, with the seven gods of luck within, were not less interesting. The steep, winding street leading to town is bordered its entire length with houses where little earthenware dolls are made and sold—a collection so cu-

In Bamboo Lands.

rious in a land of curiosities that, enticed from shop to shop, we forgot the lapse of time, until reminded by a coolie, who remarked "me catee"—a vacuity of phrase which we did not wait to investigate.

Just below the entrance to the hotel grounds are the quarters of the kurumayas, and the faithful men were always on duty at whatever hour required. They have a look of comfort and good-humor which is a Japanese trait. I had hired one for my sojourn and soon grew to like his pleasant, homely face, and felt so secure in his kindly care that I frequently rode for miles at night behind his fleet feet. A cab-horse might run away or go lame, but with a sure-footed man it is different. Just before I left Kyōto he introduced me to his pretty young wife and children, who lived cosily and happily on his father's farm near Ōtsu. One ought to see something of this old civilization to understand what peace of mind means.

"The wisest, happiest, of our kind are they
That ever walk content with nature's way."

Tea-houses and photograph galleries edge the lane that connects with the main Kyōto thoroughfare, and at the foot are numerous show-tents and an irrepressible troop of monkeys, that, in spite of our liberal efforts supplemented by those of the general public, continued ever in a state of imminent starvation. A famous cherry-tree, planted three hundred years ago, stands in the open space, that swarmed with children at play. Kite-flying (bamboo frames covered with tough paper),

KIYOMIZU-DERA.

Kyoto.

top-spinning, battledore and shuttlecock, and other familiar games were the favorites. Little girls of seven or eight years, dressed like their elders and powdered and rouged, played at games with babies on their backs; and smaller ones staggered under their loads, or carried a big doll strapped on in a similar fashion.

When a baby is seven days old its name is officially registered, and on that day the family eats festival rice cooked with red beans, to bring good luck. The boys' heads are all shaved, except funny little tufts on the top or back of the ears. No matter where one goes, the extraordinary number of children one sees is remarkable; and I rather liked them, as they are usually fat and well-nourished, quiet and well-behaved, and a never-failing source of amusement.

The nation has a fondness for birds and insects as well as for flowers. Buddha forbade their destruction, and no Japanese child would kill or torment the smallest created thing.

An open space, still farther down the avenue, was the stand of a noisy crowd of kurumayas, who were determined we should not walk. They were even more importunate in their demands than their kindred in Yokohama. We tolerated them for some days, and each day the clamor grew louder, until at last they surrounded us and interrupted our exercise. Things had gone too far—we hesitated, summoned an official, and left them to snarl.

At the foot of the hill the Kamo-gawa River, crossed by numerous bridges, intersects the city. It has the same habit of shrinking common to all on the island, and at that season was

In Bamboo Lands.

but a narrow stream with much of its pebbly bed free from water. On these long stretches of sand tons of edible seaweed were hung on lines to dry, and quantities of cotton cloth were spread out to bleach. These two are important industries. Seaweed is a favorite article of diet, and after being

WASH-DAY.

dried is carried into the interior, where it forms part of every meal among the peasantry. The kimona of the poorer class is made entirely of cotton tacked or basted together, and when washed is taken to pieces, and each piece, after being slightly stiffened, is stretched on a board to dry.

In close proximity to the modern English railway station is the ancient twin temple of Nishi Hongwanji. Our guide

Kyoto.

pointed to a large ichō tree in the courtyard, and told us with a solemn air of belief that in case of fire in the neighborhood the temple would not require the services of the "department" —the tree would protect it by the discharge of volumes of water. We were allowed to enter after the coolies had tied over our shoes blue cotton socks—ill-fitting things that would not stay on; and we had constantly to retrace our steps to recover a missing gaiter. A priest appeared to show us around, and at his request we placed our names upon the temple register. The central hall is very plain, but the walls and columns of the large rooms at either end are heavy with gilt and ornamented with lotus-flowers and leaves. The kakemonos there displayed are its chief glory. On the dark-blue ground of these mural hangings—nearly two centuries old—prayers to Amida are inscribed. These, with the portraits of successive high priests, are magnificent specimens from the brush of that celebrated school of painters which originated early in 1400. Gold plays an important rôle in Japanese art, and is lavishly used in the nave; the folding doors, the sliding screens, the panels, and frieze are richly gilded and decorated with winter scenes and pierced woodwork. The chancel glistened faintly in the half-light, and the priest held tapers that we might see to better effect the elaborately carved black-lacquered altar, the handsome gold shrine, and wonderful carvings of the ceiling. The ornaments of the high altar are two candlesticks, two vases filled with natural flowers, and an ancient bronze incense burner.

The smaller temple is connected with the larger by a cov-

In Bamboo Lands.

ered passage, and its decorations, much faded and discolored, are also the work of famous artists. The painting on one panel is very cleverly executed; there is also a fine sliding screen, on whose gold ground a Kano had painted a peach-tree in full blossom, and perched among its sprays are a peacock and peahen of jewelled plumage. The golden shrine contains an image of Amida surrounded by a halo.

Our permit gave admission to the State apartments of a hundred rooms, whose walls are overspread with gold-leaf. The effect was beautiful and bewildering. We were taken into room after room, where the talent of the Japanese artist is shown in rich designs of bamboo on gold ground, fans, peacocks, the lovely blossoms of cherry and plum trees, the royal flower of Japan, the snow-white camellia, the graceful wistaria, and Chinese landscapes treated with infinite grace and skill. We gazed at these superb decorations until weary, and were relieved when shown into the garden, exquisitely laid out with small lakes that seemed made to float paper boats, little ponds of gold and silver fish, tiny stone bridges, and moss-grown lanterns, paths that end in dense shrubbery, trees grown to great height as nature intended, and pines dwarfed by art. The garden, enclosed by high walls, is solitary and silent in the midst of a crowded city. The summer palace of Hideyoshi, a small pavilion in a remote corner of the grounds, is its chief charm. We ascended to the upper gallery and looked down upon that retreat of perfect sweetness far from the noise of busy streets.

In the temple enclosure stands the theological seminary

Kyoto.

for the education of Buddhist priests, some of whom are to be sent as missionaries to Christian countries; for, as the monk remarked in perfect English: "If you send men to convert us, why should we not pay you the same attention, as we know

BUDDHIST PRIESTS.

our religion to be more ancient and more logical than yours?" Not wishing to be entangled in erudite discussions, we did not attempt to deny the statement, and began to muse upon the new order of things when our religious training should be in the hands of a teacher of Buddhism.

Japan is now without a State religion, although a recent

In Bamboo Lands.

attempt was made in parliament to make the Christian the religion of the State, and failed because it was declared illogical. There are as many Buddhist sects as Christian, and missionaries have gained a certain advantage from that fact, in explaining the differences in forms and ceremonies of denominations represented there, as all foreign churches are erected side by side on land conceded by the government. Resident Europeans, by their irreligion, and the number of Eurasians or half-castes—unfortunate children of Christian fathers—at the open ports do much to retard the spread of Christianity, and travellers, in the rush of sight-seeing, neglect their own places of worship to visit heathen shrines. It is a trying condition of affairs.

Buddhist temples are always open, night and day, throughout the year; and some of the most wonderful temples in the world are those in which Buddha is worshipped. In Japan alone there are about seventy thousand; the old faith has been sleeping but is by no means dead, and it is not surprising that a new can gain but little headway. To study Buddhism is to be entangled in a network of metaphysics; to solve its tangled "mysteries" is to find that its highest end is to enter finally and forever into the "state of Nirvana, the essence of Buddha"—cessation of sorrow, utter annihilation, complete extinction, perpetual rest. Shintō (a Chinese word meaning the "Way of the Gods"), the ancient religion of the empire, prescribes the reverence of the Mikado as supreme sovereign, and of his maternal ancestress, the sun goddess, as the chief of its deities. It is merely ancestor worship, and its outgrowth

Kyoto.

is the veneration of parents. The priests are allowed to marry. Religion in Japan is a study by itself, a subject to which the natives seem to be rather indifferent; and one religion more or less is of little account with a nation so intensely materialistic.

We re-entered the temple in time to be present at a Buddhist service—a gorgeous and impressive ceremonial. It was difficult to realize we were not in a Christian church. The magnificent high altar with its candlesticks and lighted candles, the draped figures of Buddha with halos on their heads, vases with freshly gathered flowers, the burning incense that pervaded the sanctuary, the ringing of sweet-toned bells, the embroidered vestments, and the richness and splendor of the

SHINTŌ PRIEST.

ritual formed a combination curiously similar. Did the European borrow from the Asiatic? "Too much has been made of rituals and vestments," "empty forms and ceremonies," and religion is confounded with creed. Erasmus says: "The world is choked with opinions which are but human after all. . . . Money must be spent to buy organs, and teach boys to

In Bamboo Lands.

squeal. . . . If they want music, let them sing psalms like rational beings, and not too many of those. . . . Theologians are never tired of discussing the modes of sin, whether it be a privation in the soul or a spot on the soul . . . We dispute how the Father differs from the Son, and both from the Holy Ghost, whether it be a difference of fact or a difference of relation, and how three can be one when neither of the three is the other."

It was an hour past noon when we left the temple and made our way to Higashi Hongwanji, through streets of shops where ecclesiastical goods are made and sold. The fronts were crowded with shrines, idols, household gods, religious knickknacks, and all the gorgeous paraphernalia of Buddhist worship. The devout Japanese have plenty of things to adore. It was interesting to watch the manufacture of deities, grotesquely represented in wood or bronze, and the shrines in brass and gold-leaf for use in private houses. It seemed strange to us that these deluded souls could address prayers to an idol made to order under their own eyes. Incense, too, is used in large quantities, and shops for the sale of it are separate and numerous.

Higashi Hongwanji, founded on the site of a former temple, was destroyed by fire in 1867, and is now being rebuilt. Begun in 1868, this remarkable structure has taken all these years to construct, and thus far eight millions of dollars have been expended upon it. Buddhism has had a wonderful revival, as is evidenced by the popular enterprise that built the huge edifice. Subscriptions were sent from all parts of the

Kyoto.

country, timber and other materials were furnished by the neighboring provinces, and the poor have given their labor. Women of all ages cut off their hair and sent it to be woven into ropes of every size, from a small cord to a big cable. They were used to hoist stone and timber, and now lie in great coils on the portico, to be preserved as relics. The structure was greatly encumbered by an enormous scaffolding, formed of poles tied together by ropes that appeared insecure enough to alarm us as we stood under it to watch the carpenters and the wood-carvers at work. This noble edifice has been built entirely by hand-labor, without machinery of any kind; and scores of men and women stood ready to assist in placing huge logs in position. Who can dare to assert, in presence of this work, that Buddhism is dying out? The building is of wood and the interior is finished with keaki, the Japanese elm, much prized and used generally for the nave of temples. It is one of the finest of the native trees, and grows to an enormous size. The only ornaments we saw were the four magnificent bronze lanterns that stand in the courtyard.

The fatiguing day was at an end, and our veranda was never more restful than when we reclined in luxury at cup-of-tea time to watch the sunset on the mountains, and, enveloped in rugs, to enjoy a half-hour nap before dinner.

The weather continued fine, to our great delight, and my comrade suggested that we spend the following day in the country. She chose the excursion to Uji, the most famous of the Japanese tea districts, a ride of eleven miles by kuruma

In Bamboo Lands.

over good roads. It was a beautiful day; the air was warm with not a breath of wind stirring, the sun shone brightly, overhead was the blue sky, and we were soon beyond the limits of the old town and riding among fields that stretch over the plain without a fence to mar the landscape. We stopped twice at tea-houses to give the coolies a short rest, and gathered great armfuls of scarlet lilies and bought shoots of bamboo to decorate the carriages, not foreseeing in what a plight we should find ourselves. In possession of the long-coveted foliage, our happiness was complete as we rode into Uji with the feathery tips waving about us. Then, as a bolt out of the blue, and without knowing the cause, we were stopped by an official, who demanded our passports, opened them, and pointed angrily to a certain line. We glanced at the translation and learned that we were accused of "injuring plants," and were answerable for a breach of the law. I can imagine what a forlorn appearance we must have presented at that moment, as, surrounded by an excited crowd, we waited for our stupid guide to explain to the not less stupid official that the bamboo had been paid for with good, honest silver. Another five minutes was consumed in appeasing the villagers, who could not comprehend why foreigners should be allowed to destroy shrubs to adorn kurumas. Peace was restored at last, and we were allowed to proceed after the offending branches had been torn away and hidden under the seats. A great stir had been raised and all for nothing. We pushed forward with lighter hearts.

The village of Uji lies on the banks of the broad Yodagwaa

Kyoto.

River, environed by plantations famous for producing the finest tea in Japan. Tea-raising in this district dates from 1291, and must be added to the list of good things brought from China by Buddhist priests in A.D. 805. There were no facto-

TEA HOUSE.

ries for drying and selling the tea; each family worked by itself in a small way. We went to several tiny homes, and saw the leaves spread out on mats, drying in the sun. Some grades of tea bring high prices—notably the Gyokuro, which sells for six dollars a pound. Our inefficient guide, anxious to redeem his reputation, induced us to visit an old Buddhist

In Bamboo Lands.

temple founded in 1052, and noted for its kakemonos, scrolls, and relics of Yorimasa—a warrior of the twelfth century, who, after "prodigies of valor," hard pressed by his enemies, committed harakiri at the age of seventy-five. Phœnix Hall, in the same grounds, is an ancient building, reproduced at the World's Fair in 1893.

The day was too lovely to waste in dingy interiors, and we hastened on to spend the noontide hour at one of the many tea-houses that overlook the river. The tea-houses of Uji are ideal and are ceaselessly represented by Japanese art. The architecture is unique, the finish artistic, the broad balconies afford fine views up and down the river, and their gardens are as pretty as native taste can make them. Clumps of bamboo and maples with sprays of scarlet and gold brightened the hill-slopes, and up the deep gorge ferns and mosses overgrew the cliffs. We chose one of these inviting inns and removed our shoes before ascending to an upper room, whose polished floor was so exquisite we feared to mar its shining surface, being quite as unwilling to walk over it as to step on a silken train in boots besmeared with mud. We had provided ourselves with a lunch, as the traveller soon learns, through experience, not to trust to ordinary Japanese food. The little waitresses—I cannot state how many, as they all looked alike—arranged the repast on a table that looked coarse and out of place in that gem-like room. The tea was delicious and brewed to perfection, as the Japanese are tea epicures. The water for making the beverage is heated but never allowed to boil, and after remaining on the leaves for a moment, until it be-

TEA HARVEST.

Kyoto.

comes a greenish straw color, the infusion is poured off, or the result would be bitter.

The balcony afforded fine views up the gorge where the river breaks through the hills, and over the acres of tea-plants just coming into bloom. The myriads of white blossoms twinkled over the fields like snowflakes thereon sprinkled. The plant is a camellia, and lovely when covered with flowers, but provokingly devoid of fragrance, especially in that small empire; for, as a witty writer on Japan has said: "There is a mistake somewhere, and the result is that in one of the most beautiful and fertile countries in the world the flowers have no scent, the birds no song, and the fruit and vegetables no flavor."

Our curiosity had been aroused to see a Japanese ferry, and a short walk up the stream gave us the desired opportunity. It was operated in a primitive way. On each bank of the river a pole was securely fixed in the ground, and stretched between them was a stout rope. A man at the stern steered the boat, while a second ferried it along by hand-over-hand motions on the cord. As business was dull that afternoon, we were ferried over and back for several trips; and if the men in charge enjoyed their earnings half as much as we did the rides, we parted mutually satisfied. Then we started back to Kyōtō. We took boat down the river to Fushima, celebrated as the residence of St. Francis Xavier, who landed at Kagoshima, on the island of Kyūshū, on the 15th of August, 1549, and began his missionary activity among the Japanese. Here our kurumas awaited us, and we were soon dashing over the road

In Bamboo Lands.

on our return. After the unpleasant incident of the morning, the feathery beauties caused no further disturbance, and they festooned the balcony outside for many a day.

The palace of the Mikado and the castle of the Shōgun are considered the most attractive sights in Kyōtō. We had reserved the visit for a rainy day which came not; so, armed cap-à-pie with permit, passports, guide-book, and small change, we were set down before one of the six gates in the wall of mud and plaster that encloses the palace grounds. The sentry examined the papers before allowing us to cross the spacious courtyard to an irregular group of dark buildings that cover twenty-six acres. Externally the palace is unattractive and without pretensions to architectural beauty, entirely opposed to foreign ideas of a royal residence; but its internal decorations enjoy great repute. Visitors, on arrival, enter by the gate of the "August Kitchen," and are shown into a room furnished with bright-colored European carpets of startling pattern and chairs upholstered with magenta, that most detestable of all colors. Names were registered, cotton socks adjusted, and, escorted by two court officials, we began the inspection of a series of cold rooms without furniture or any means of heating them. The first suite of apartments—used only on state occasions or for festivals of the ancient religion—were covered with exquisite matting. In one room a portion of the floor is made of cement; each morning this was sprinkled with sand, that the Mikado, according to prescribed form, might worship his ancestors without descending to the ground. The throne was draped with rich white, black, and red silks.

Kyoto.

We were next shown into a great hall used for coronation ceremonies, the New Year's audience, and on other state occasions. The panels were originally decorated with paintings of Chinese sages, the work of a noted artist of the ninth century; unfor-

THE PALACE OF THE MIKADO.

tunately many of the originals destroyed by fire had been replaced by copies. In the centre of the room is the raised dais, with canopy of beautiful white silk decorated with a pattern representing "the bark of an aged pine-tree." The stools at either side are rests for the imperial insignia, the Mirror, the Sword, and the Crystal, that have been handed down by generations of successive Emperors. The mirror is the emblem of

In Bamboo Lands.

justice, the sword of power, and the crystal of virtue. In ancient times the mirror was kept in the imperial palace, but later was removed to the temples of Ise, where a shrine was erected for it. When the Emperor sees in this mirror his imperial person, descended in an unbroken line from his ancestress Ama-terasu, the Sun goddess, he is supposed to be reminded of the ancestral commandment to love the people as his own family.

The descent to the court is by eighteen steps, each of which corresponds to a grade of rank into which the nobility were divided, ranging from those who must remain on the ground to the highest, who could ascend and enter the royal presence. Passing through a corridor, we were shown the Emperor's study with shelves and recesses of lacquer-work for books and writing-materials. Near by is a theatre to which the imperial household resorted to witness the Nō performances—a kind of lyric drama recited by two persons in a dramatic manner and attended only by the aristocracy.

We were next shown into a charming suite of eleven rooms where the Mikados for six centuries had lived and died secluded from their families and the world, seeing nothing but minute representations of the empire over which they ruled. The royal bed-chamber was so surrounded by apartments that it was impossible for one to approach His Majesty without the knowledge of his guards. All these rooms are ornamented with paintings by competent Japanese artists. Lacquer and choice woods are lavishly used; on dead-gold ground, scenes from nature are depicted; a wall-design represents lakes and

Kyoto.

rivers overgrown with rushes, among which song-birds flutter; another, forest scenes with groups of animals; and the panels of a third display flowers, fruits, birds, and insects worthy the brush of a Landseer. We had passed through all these courts, corridors, and halls without seeing a human being and without hearing a sound—all was dreary and deserted. The present Emperor lived but for a short period in the old palace, as he was but sixteen years of age when his rights were restored and his residence changed to Tōkyō.

We next visited the Castle or Nijō Palace, externally much like that at Nagoya, protected by broad moats and massive walls with turrets at the angles. This mighty fortress was built by the Shōgun Ieyasu in 1601 as a residence when he visited Kyōtō. It was here the Mikado, in 1868, "met the Council of State, and in their presence swore to grant a deliberate assembly and to decide all measures by public opinion." In later years, while occupied by the prefecture of Kyōtō, many of its antique works of art were defaced or destroyed. Since it has been reserved for a royal palace, to which the Emperor occasionally comes for a change of air, much has been effected in restoring it to its former splendor, and the imperial crest —the sixteen-petalled chrysanthemum—has in many instances replaced the three asarum leaves of the Shōgun.

We entered the enclosure that surrounds it by the great gate, heavy with carvings and clamped with bronze-work that deserves close attention. Ancient pines, interesting relics of a past age, flourish in the courtyard. The inner gate is still more gorgeous in its wealth of gold and colors, and curious

In Bamboo Lands.

carvings by a renowned engraver of Japan, the son of a peasant, who became a wood-carver by chance and raised the trade from simple carpenter-work to a place among the fine arts. The castle is a rambling one-story building with immense rooms without either furniture or mats—furniture they never had, and vandalism destroyed the mats. The walls are incrusted with gold and silver leaf. Enormous paintings on gold ground by artists of skill represent baskets of flowers, fans, trees of various kinds, animals feeding, and birds in flight. The wide friezes of pierced woodwork for ventilation are exquisitely fine. In one set, the effect is striking and beautiful: minutely carved peacocks are displayed on one side and perfectly outlined peonies on the other.

The Hall of Audience is provided with two levels. On the higher one the Shōgun sat in gorgeous state surrounded by his court to receive the daimyōs with their glittering trains, who prostrated themselves on the floor below. This apartment is decorated with enormous plum-trees and a wealth of gold-leaf and the many fine-metal crests of the Shōgun that have been suffered to remain. The panels of the reception-room are charmingly ornamented with paintings of cherry-trees in full blossom, and many other details were noticed, among which was a bit of antique cloisonné. We were shown through endless suites of rooms, rich in decorative screens that we examined and admired until exhausted with so much of history and of art. Not once in our tour of the Castle did either officer or guide mention the Emperor. Everything of interest is connected with the Shōguns, those great Tycoons who spared

Kyoto.

no expense in rearing palaces and tombs the finest in the empire, as monuments for all time of their superior abilities.

The longer one remains in Kyōtō the more satisfying it becomes: one finds how uninterruptedly the old life of the people

STREET IN KYOTO.

is going on, notwithstanding the influx of European ideas. Besides the many fine establishments of costly goods, there are streets without number of curio-shops crowded with relics of ancient times. It requires hours of patient search to select from a mass of articles without name or price those that are really valuable as acquisitions. In our endless wanderings

In Bamboo Lands.

through narrow streets, escorted by a crowd of all ages, we saw at every step curious scenes and interesting little customs we should never have heard of had we been in charge of a guide. Guides are an indispensable luxury at times, but they chill one's enthusiasm.

The houses are narrow, the shops occupy the whole front, and they are generally so close together they touch each other. The salesman, who sits in his shop warming his hands over a hibachi (charcoal-brazier) and smoking his everlasting pipe, shows his good-will by making the usual salutation; and it matters not whether the customer be a large investor or a tiresome creature who inquires the price of every article and buys nothing—he is equally courteous to all. The moment we were seated the crowd gazed curiously, intent on finding out all about us and our business. Our conversation could not have been edifying, as it was confined mostly to " Ikura?" (" How much?")—a word impossible to dispense with in the country, or to dispel when one leaves it. Time is of no importance in Japan and bargaining at a curio-shop is no light matter, since the shopkeepers ask foreigners a price much larger than the sum they mean to take or than you mean to pay—if you understand their methods—for life has taught them "to truckle and trick like the rest of us." They appear to believe that travellers are easily imposed upon; but if the customer be wise and feign indifference, in nine cases out of ten he will get the article, regardless of the original price demanded. He makes great use of the soraban, an instrument enclosing rows of beads sliding on thick wires—a trap to catch the unwary; at the same time

Kyoto.

while preparing to exploit you, he draws in his breath in that curious faint whistle, to indicate that he is a slave to your wishes. My English friend had given me a list of real antiques—a medicine box, an incense burner, a folding candlestick, an embroidered scroll, several small ornaments, and a

BAMBOO WARE FOR SALE.

Japanese clock of the kind in use before they came into contact with time-keepers of European make. There are many varieties, but all record the moments without a pointer, rotating on an axis; the scale and figures are arranged in a fashion resembling a Fahrenheit thermometer more than anything else, the pointer or hand being attached to a rod which continu-

In Bamboo Lands.

ally slides down the "time-tube," thus marking the hour and the minutes as it slowly but imperceptibly falls toward the "weight-house." We found a bronze candlestick so curiously constructed it took months to discover what it was made for. I was disappointed in not securing an ancient map of Japan, like one I had seen representing that little empire as occupying the centre and greater part of the universe, with other countries ranged about it as vassals. Japan is almost denuded of real curios, and, though our collection is still incomplete, the search afforded an endless, agreeable, and profitable occupation.

The cars took us to Ōtsu at the foot of Lake Biwa, a fine sheet of water forty-five miles long—the largest and prettiest of the Japanese lakes. On the north and west sides it is walled in by mountains covered with forests; small farms and villages line the opposite shores. The lake, which is very deep at some points and abounds in fish, was made still more picturesque by small trading-steamers and fishing-boats that ply its waters. There is a tradition that the sacred mountain of Fujiyama was formed in a single night by an earthquake; the depression of Lake Biwa was produced simultaneously, and the natives believe there is still a connection between the two.

Ōtsu is a flourishing town, with an unenviable reputation as the spot where the attempt was made to assassinate the Czarevitch—now Czar Nicholas II.—during his journey around the world. He reached Kyōtō on May 9th, and two days later his party made an excursion to the classic Lake Biwa. They had seen the lake and paid a short visit to the prefectural office,

Kyoto.

and were prepared to see the outskirts of the town in kurumas. The streets of Ōtsu were well lined with police, and as the party rode along a Japanese guard, Tsuda Sanzo, drew his sword and directed a powerful blow at the Czarevitch—inflicting two cuts on his forehead. His sun helmet broke the force of the blow, and Prince George of Greece, his travelling companion, with admirable presence of mind felled the would-be assassin with a stout walking-stick, and threw himself on the man before he had time to inflict another wound. With the aid of the police, the assailant was finally secured and afterward sentenced to imprisonment for life. The most mysterious rumors gained currency: it was said that Sanzo was a half-crazy fanatic of the Samurai class, noted for their hatred of Europeans; also, that he was a Nihilist belonging to Russia in the Japanese police service. In any case, the Grand Duke very luckily escaped with only two slight cuts.

His Majesty and the court went into mourning; the Emperor travelled over two hundred miles to visit the wounded Prince; the Empress kept her bed for weeks and spent the time in weeping; and placards announced that the reception and banquet to be given for the Czarevitch were indefinitely postponed. "Some grim old Samurai showed their feelings about the occurrence in a less gentle manner. The high official intrusted with the safety of the Czarevitch at Ōtsu received, by express, a fine sword and a stern letter bidding him prove his manhood and his regret like a Samurai, by performing harakiri immediately." The Prince shortened his stay in Japan and returned to St. Petersburg by way of Siberia, and this portion of his

In Bamboo Lands.

travels is believed to have had no small influence on the construction of the Trans-Siberian Railway. The zeal for Western civilization grew colder after that catastrophe.

A short ride from the station through queer little streets brought us to the foot of the hill dedicated to the goddess Kwannon. The view from the summit is so fine one feels amply repaid for the ascent. We hailed the sight with pleasure; the broad expanse of Lake Biwa spread out at our feet; and Hiei-zan, the priests' mountain, towering high above the sea and the little ships, threw long shadows over its surface. The Buddhist temple of Miidera has few ornaments; but its storehouses are rich in priceless antique art of lacquer, embroidery, and brocade.

Among the groves are numerous shrines well storied with many a thrilling legend. One, in connection with an enormous iron bowl we saw by the roadside, relates that the vessel was once filled with soup that an individual consumed and thereby gained strength to carry it to the top of the sacred mountain. There seemed to be little foundation for the legend, except the reality of the bowl; but what his object was in taking it up there, and how it got back again, did not appear, and this story, like others we listened to, was a tissue of nonsense.

After coming down we took kurumas to the village of Karasaki, famous for its pine-tree, whose branches, supported by a trellis, number four hundred and average two hundred and fifty feet in length. The trunk is carefully sheltered from rain by a roof over the top, and the decayed spots are filled

PINE TREE AT KARASAKI.

Kyoto.

with plaster. It has the reputation of being the oldest tree in the country, and has been worshipped for ages. It stands on a sandy point protected by stone-faced embankments, and, like the immense banyan tree in the gardens at Calcutta, is remarkable for the great area covered by one plant. This is the place for picnics; there were benches under the tree, and a party of natives were having their noonday repast under this canopy of drooping boughs. It was too suggestive, however, of bygone festivities to suit us, and we returned to Ōtsu, the kurumayas having trotted there and back without the smallest sense of fatigue.

We lunched at the tea-house of Minaraitei on the lake. The dining-room, which occupied the whole upper floor, was open front and back, affording lovely views over the water and the town, and was made still more attractive by hanging scrolls, pines, and potted shrubs. We enjoyed greatly the freshly caught fish, that on this occasion were cooked and not eaten with chop-sticks.

After a pleasant hour there, we rode around the south shore to the long bridge of Seta. The scenery was extremely pretty—the lake glistened to the left, and to the right the hills, green with coniferae, sloped to the shore. A bridge has existed there from prehistoric times, and the legend connected with an earlier structure is very characteristic of Japanese fairy tales. The hero was "My Lord Bag o' Rice," who had a very remarkable experience with a sea-serpent twenty feet long and an exciting battle beneath the waters of the lake with a centipede over a mile in length, and enjoyed

In Bamboo Lands.

happiness and great wealth ever after, as a reward of his prowess.

A short distance farther on is the village of Ishiyama-dera and its temple, located on the mountain-side. The beautifying of the grounds—a fine example of a temple garden—has been the chief object of the monks, and they are lovely. Limpid streams glide between grassy banks, rustic bridges span diminutive lakes, shrubs grow on rocks of fantastic shape, and pines grace the lawn. From sunny nooks and spaces with clusters of shrubs high up among the maples, a fair prospect expands before the eye over garden and lake.

We returned to Kyōtō by kuruma, along the much-travelled Tōkaidō, that runs through a pass among the hills. Before our advent, the wild-flowers grew by the wayside unmolested; we piled our little cabs high with blue, white, and yellow beauties, assisted by the coolies who vied with each other in scaling steep places to gather specimens above our reach. The Japanese love of nature does not extend to these unassuming plants, and we were delighted that our passports had also neglected them. The road was thronged with kurumas, people on foot, and man-carts loaded with merchandise. These carts are usually drawn by two men, aided by two others who push from behind, all four keeping up a hoarse guttural cry to encourage each other. We also noticed several family affairs: the man in the shafts, the wife pushing in the rear with an infant lashed to her back, other children trudging along at the side, all seeming to be enjoying themselves. One sees much of industrious poverty in Japan, where the poor form the vast

Kyoto.

majority of the population. On again, gradually descending, we neared Kyōtō at sunset, riding through temple grounds just as the bells of Nanzenji and Chion-in rang out their surpassingly sweet tones on the evening air.

There is nothing about the exterior of the great silk-shops to distinguish them from the dwellings of the poor; all are alike of wood, and unpainted. We stopped before one of these unpretentious buildings, entered by a small door, and were conducted through passages and anterooms to an apartment in the rear, containing great cabinets of antique lacquer filled with art-work and tables loaded with rich silks, brocades, velvets, and silk crêpes; satin screens superbly embroidered in gold, with designs of wild ducks, winter scenes, sprays of cherry and plum blossoms, iris-flowers, the queenly rose, the sacred lotus, storks in flight, deer feeding under forest shadows, and symbols of good fortune, were an important part of the stock. The show-room opened upon a garden where, when surfeited with art, we could enjoy nature. This small yard of tidy flower-beds and neatly kept paths was beautified by quaintly trimmed pines three or four feet high, blossoming trees, a vine-covered trellis, the usual stone lantern and pool of fish, and a retreat used for tea-drinking, capable of holding two persons only. We dawdled away whole afternoons in this elegant interior, this home of art. The proprietor, in addition to other courtesies, invariably served tea and little pleasantries of sweets and fruit. A gentleman of our party was an enthusiastic buyer, and in one recklessly extravagant session we were regaled with hot sake, poured from a fine bronze pot.

In Bamboo Lands.

Hot sake—a magical intoxicant, an evil to be avoided! It was well for him he was temperate, else he might have fallen into the bog and purchased the entire stock.

Embroidery, with other arts, was imported from China by the priests; but with the Japanese art is an inspiration, and they have invested their work with their own exquisite taste. Curiously enough, the first noted artist in embroidery was a Buddhist nun, but now all the finest specimens are the work of men and boys. We were taken into the work-rooms and shown pieces, still far from completed, upon which the embroiderers had been at work for months. They receive ridiculously small pay, and it is not surprising they lose their sight early in life, for the intricate patterns and delicate shading would try the strongest eyes.

The following morning was one of anticipation and of disappointment. One of my fellow-travellers took us far out of our way to visit the monastery of Kenninji, situated in a park that extends to the left of the town. When we arrived, we alighted and were taken by a priest through room after room containing nothing whatever. After exhausting that form of entertainment, he volunteered the information that a fair for the sale of old clothes would be held there the following day. These monks have a reputation for profound Buddhistic lore, but there was no religious sentiment in that remark. We thought him something of a practical joker, and, as we were rather sensitive about our own travel-stained garments, we took kurumas and went on our way.

The temple of Kōdaiji is dedicated to Hideyoshi, who be-

Kyoto.

gan life as a peasant, rose by his talents to a position of influence, and became practically ruler of Japan under the title of Regent. His ambition was to become Emperor of the whole East. He sent armies to Korea in 1542 and ruined that country; he also planned the conquest of China, but death overtook him in 1598, and his enterprise came to naught. He is known as the Napoleon of Japan. His infant son Hideyori succeeded him, but was overpowered by Ieyasu, who founded the Tokugawa dynasty of Shōguns, that remained in power until 1868.

The greater number of the buildings have been destroyed by fire, but the grounds that extend up the terraced hillside are shaded by ancient oaks and elms and very beautiful. The place is full of absorbing interest in connection with Hideyoshi. The apartments contain some famous gold screens and other antiques; Founder's Hall has panels painted by illustrious artists of the Kano school; in the mortuary chapel is a figure of Hideyoshi seated in a shrine of rich black lacquer, and they still point out the spot where he used to sit and gaze at the moon. There are many beautiful carved and lacquered relics and old bronzes worthy of careful examination, but we had been taken by storm. An acolyte of the mature age of seven met us at the gate, and engrossed our whole attention. He at once began shouting, in high, shrill tones, Japanese words that we did not understand, but which we supposed to be an explanation of the place and its contents. Our sense of the comic was too great, and at first we felt inclined to laugh at the serious expression on the boy's face; but while we rambled about and looked at everything, he clung to us persistently. We cried

In Bamboo Lands.

"Leave us in peace!" beat the floor with sticks, studied the guide-book, and essayed by every means in our power to rid ourselves of the chattering magpie, but made no more impression on that aspiring spirit than on the bronze images of the altar. At last, there came into my head one of those bright ideas that occasionally assail the dullest mind, and I handed him a fee. A fatal error—it but encouraged him to greater efforts! He had the precocious air of an embryo actor reciting one of those long-drawn-out dramas that begin in the morning and last until midnight. We had stirred up a hornet's nest—to silence him was impossible, and to escape being talked to death we abandoned the spot.

From the noisy experience at Kōdaiji, we found refuge in the quiet elegance of Ikedas' shop, where the finest specimens of cloisonné, satsuma, damascene, bronze, and lacquer are displayed. A cabinet valued at ten thousand dollars, decorated with gold and richly lacquered, was but one of the many gems of art in the collection. The articles were arranged on tables and shelves, with ample space for examination. We wondered, admired, and enjoyed. Japan, even in her art, offers us that which we most desire in travel—novelty; and there is nothing to offend the eye. The race has too much good sense and innate refinement to daub their art-work and fill public prints with representations of the nude female form.

To still further gratify our curiosity, the owner kindly invited us to visit the factory in an adjoining building. For making damascene, the iron is first cast in the required shape; the surface is then roughened with hammer and chisel; then

A SHOP.

Kyoto.

bits of gold and silver are hammered in in patterns; and, lastly, the piece is lacquered and fired. The process of making cloisonné is equally interesting. The article is first hammered into symmetry out of copper; the design is drawn on it with ink; then a network of brass is soldered on to the metal foundation and the interstices filled with enamel paste in various colors, to be finally subjected to baking, rubbing, and polishing until the surface is perfectly hard and smooth. The process is so extremely delicate that often many specimens are destroyed before a flawless one is produced. Each separate part of the work is done by one artist, who knows nothing of other parts. Their skill excels in the minuteness of detail, and it is surprising what artistic effects they produce with the simplest of instruments.

Except for the ascent of Fujiyama, our next excursion to the rapids of the Katsuragawa was the most adventurous we made in Japan. The weather still favored us, and the ride of fifteen miles by kurumas with two men each across the mountain range to Hōzu, where we took boats, was delightful. The scenery in these mountains is exceedingly lovely, and there can be few places where nature has so lavishly scattered her choicest treasures. The beeches and maples were magnificent; a stream wound tortuously through a rocky ravine; the breezes were spicy with delicate perfume; the faint blue of the autumn sky shone through the trees. The graceful drooping cherry-colored berries of the nightshade and the delicate maidenhair fern grew in profusion; wild asters with lavender-purple rays and yellow centres, the crimson-magenta clusters

In Bamboo Lands.

of the iron-weed, the small blue flowers of the modest self-heal, and wild chrysanthemums and other late varieties blossomed there in sunny spots.

We stopped at a small village to allow the coolies a short rest and breathing-spell on their long uphill journey. Every house was a shop, and the mystery was where the buyers came from, for, with the exception of our kurumayas, I saw no purchasers. In some, all kinds of food were displayed—fish, rice, beans, and seaweed predominating; in others hats, rain-coats, and sandals of straw, and many small articles of bamboo and lacquer were for sale. We could see the domestic arrangements and everything else that was going on inside; and the small garden in the rear made a pleasing background to the quaint picture. The shopkeeper was smoking at ease among his wares, a young woman was seated with her hair-dresser busy at work, others were sewing or cooking—they understand cooking rice to perfection—and in one little home the family were at dinner, each with his separate table a foot square and a foot high. The table and the little bowls for rice, soup, fish, and other food were all lacquered. The natives seemed to have plenty of leisure and always suspended work the moment we appeared at the door, eyeing us with quite as much curiosity as we did them. The packhorses we met on the way were the most hopelessly depressed looking creatures imaginable, burdened with curiously shaped cargoes, so huge that little of the unfortunate animals was visible except the head and legs. Charms are tied about their necks, they are shod with straw sandals to protect the feet on stony roads, and are charged with

Kyoto.

having some spirit—but how can they display it, when loaded until they look like hay mounds on four legs? After a life of toil comes the reward: they are buried like human beings in cemeteries devoted to them. The leader had the same stolid

A FAMILY DINNER-PARTY.

resignation reflected in his face as he trudged along, leading his quadruped by a rope.

Arrived at Hōzu we embarked in flat-bottomed boats twenty feet long, kurumas, coolies, and all, for the ride down-stream of fifteen miles. There are twenty-two rapids, and the descent usually takes about two hours. The walls of the canyon through which the clear rushing stream has cut its way are al-

In Bamboo Lands.

most vertical and wooded to their summits. The river immediately enters this magnificent mountain gorge, the excitement begins, and the tourist has an opportunity for testing his nerve. In the savage grandeur of the scenery, the water rushing in whitening foam over the rocky bed of the torrent, and the fleet and boisterous frolic there was infinite exhilaration. So closely do the mountains hem in the stream that, on looking up, it seemed as if there were no outlet to the place, and at several abrupt turns around jutting crags as if nothing could prevent one's being dashed to pieces on huge boulders. The echoes, as if the angry spirits of the mountains were let loose, were sublime. It requires consummate skill, practice, and coolness to manage a craft in that raging torrent, which whirled the boat swiftly downward until we emerged from the gorge, gliding peacefully into still water, and our landing-place came into view. On the way down we met boatmen towing their skiffs laboriously up-stream. In the charming village of Arashiyama we picnicked on a balcony that overlooks the river, and returned to Kyōtō, but not until the long shadows of the trees warned us that it was time to leave. I should have liked to detain each hour as it passed.

The next morning came sad news of the death of two English friends, who went down in an ill-fated steamer of the Peninsular and Oriental line, in a typhoon off the Chinese coast.

Outside the present city limits, toward the northwest, is a collection of temples and gardens of more or less interest. The temple of Kitano Tenjin is a good specimen of the result of mixing the two religions; the devout may there worship

GOLDEN PAVILION, KINKAKUJI.

Kyoto.

their Shintō deities in company with the pompous ritual prescribed by Buddhism. The temple is finely located on high ground, the approach is by a massive stone torii, but the decorations are coarse and cheap, the altar is littered with idols, the avenue is lined with restaurants and show-places, and the whole effect is irreligious and uninteresting. It was pitiful, absolutely pitiful.

We hastened on to Kinkakuji, so called from the golden pavilion in the grounds. A palace was erected there by the ex-Shōgun Yoshimitsu as long ago as 1397, but nothing now remains of it. He laid out the ornamental garden after Japanese style and built the pavilion of three stories on the lake. In its prime there were fine paintings by a Kano on the ceiling; the upper story was entirely encrusted with gold-leaf and the roof crowned by a golden phœnix three feet high. The effect must have been gorgeous in the extreme, and even now, tarnished and time-beaten, it is a pretty and peaceful retreat. Here the ex-Shōgun with shaved head and priestly robes used to sit and meditate, while enjoying the pretty sheet of water covered with lotus-plants and swarming with carp. As we stood on the balcony, these silent inmates of the pool with brilliant scales and quick sense heard our voices and darted up to be fed. The intricate art of gardening is there seen to perfection—forest trees and flowering shrubs, streams, rockeries, bridges, woodland paths, summer-houses perched on knolls, and a "moon-gazing arbor"—favorite haunts of Yoshimitsu, the very "serenity of solitude." We visited the apartments, where everything about us was ancient. The screens,

In Bamboo Lands.

panels, and kakemonos three hundred years old were in a fine state of preservation and exquisite specimens of the art-work of Old Japan. In the courtyard was a curiosity: a large pine-tree has been trained in the form of a junk and gives an excellent representation. We failed to learn its age, but a priest informed us that it had been growing there for centuries. I bought a tempo, a large oblong bronze coin with a hole in the centre, intended to be strung on a string for convenience in handling. They were coined during the period A. D. 1830–1844, are worth eight rin, and are not now produced. The priests offered tea, which we accepted without waiting for the elaborate ceremony, as time was limited, and we had yet, while in the vicinity, to visit another historic spot.

We sped until we came to Daitokuji, once a magnificent temple of the Zen sect of Buddhists. It is a stately old building standing in solitary grandeur, with a distinct individuality in the religious atmosphere which surrounds it. It was quite enough to sit in the ancient temple, to breathe the air of the venerable place, full of repose to those who can receive its influences. The carvings on the gateways and the interior are wonderful, and its treasures of damask, embroidery, and lacquer are renowned for richness and beauty, and unsurpassed by any other productions of human skill. In the apartments, painters of the best school spent years in decorating the walls, panels, and screens according to antique custom. In one instance, the artist has chosen beautiful Chinese scenery and delineated it with accuracy. A very spirited picture occupies an entire wall; the subject is simple but broad, clear, and toned har-

A PINE-TREE TRAINED IN THE FORM OF A JUNK.

Kyoto.

moniously. It represents a man teaching a monkey to dance. On leaving the temple we climbed to the hilltop, where stands a shrine dedicated to Nobunaga, a deified warrior of the sixteenth century, and had views far and wide of miles of surrounding country. We stood on the heights that encircled the rich and fertile plain, a beautiful spot some miles outside the present city limits. The scene was one of incomparable loveliness, an ideal sunset picture of wooded hills and browning meadows.

Not content with the long day of sight-seeing, we turned aside to watch some peasants thatching the deep slanting roof of a farmhouse. The straw was laid on three feet thick, and secured in place by bamboo poles placed lengthwise across the beams. One often sees heavy stones placed on the roofs to keep them secure in high winds. Thatched roofs have in recent years given place to tiled ones in cities, and fires are now much less destructive.

Our permit to visit the palaces included the Imperial garden of Shugaku-in, lying at the base of Hiei-zan. We flew through miles of streets and out among the fields where the paths were only as wide as a kuruma, alighted at the gate, and were escorted by a lay brother through the spacious grounds finely situated on the mountain slope, and planted with grand old cherry and maple trees. One section, exquisitely laid out, is a faithful reflection of a landscape and a charming example of horticultural art. We saw in a small building many valuable relics of the founder, a Mikado who lived in the seventeenth century. It was one of those perfect days that we were so

In Bamboo Lands.

marvellously favored with, warm and bright, much like our Indian summer, and the walk of two miles around the grounds would have been one of unalloyed enjoyment, had not the place been infested with evil things. Snakes are protected with superstitious reverence, and to kill one is very wrong. I never saw so many outside a museum; they wriggled through the grass, sprawled on the roadway, and basked in the sunshine on the finely gravelled walks. Serpents four feet long, even though they be harmless, are not agreeable companions for an afternoon stroll. Our purely Oriental escort ignored alike the revolting reptiles and our abhorrence of them.

On our way to Ginkakuji we had a fine opportunity to see more of farm life as we rode among the grain-fields. The houses of the peasants are small and include under one broad overhanging roof both dwelling and barn. Much of the charm of rural life in our country is absent in Japan. As the people use neither milk nor meat, cattle, sheep, and swine are not seen, and the farmyards look singularly silent and deserted. The only representations of animal life are fowls, dogs, and cats with short stumpy tails, a freak of nature; the bones are all there, but not normally developed. A strong prejudice exists against the long-tailed species, as they are supposed to have power to bewitch beings, and if one chances to be born the appendage is chopped off without ceremony.

The methods of agriculture are primitive. The soil is spaded by men and women with simple instruments; hoes and mattocks are used for gardening, and short, straight knives for reaping. The fields are cultivated to the highest point, and,

A FARMER.

with constant enriching, will produce as many as three crops annually. The town scavengers collect the sewage and refuse of every house daily and sell it to the farmers, who preserve it in large tubs sunk into the ground until needed, when it is taken in wooden pails and distributed about the fields.

The peasants wear the usual shirt and short breeches of blue cotton, a bowl-shaped hat as large as an umbrella, and a fan stuck in the girdle. In wet weather they don a straw raincoat in two parts,—the upper cape tied about the neck, and the lower one fastened around the waist,—and wooden clogs four inches high held in position by a looped thong which passes between the first and second toes, to keep them out of the mire. As the average Japanese man is only five feet two inches in height, and the women are but five feet or less, these stilts are rather becoming. But fancy Europeans stalking about on them; they would look like a race of giants! Along the road, as we progressed, the path became narrow and rough; there were many places over which a wheeled vehicle could not pass, and we had to pick our way over the uneven ground and wet places, while the coolies carried the little gigs.

Arrived at the hamlet of Jōdōji-mura, we walked up the single street to Ginkakuji, one of the most noted places in the history of Kyōtō. Here the Shōgun Yoshimasa, after his abdication in 1497, laid out a fine garden with a charming background of wooded hills and built for himself a palace and silver pavilion. The apartments are dingy with age, but some good specimens of high art remain, among which is a painted figure of Yoshimasa, clad in the garb of a Buddhist priest. The

In Bamboo Lands.

clean, well-tended garden, full of interesting spots connected with his life, is a place of melancholy sweetness and repose. Trees, lakes, bridges and rocks—all are distinguished by names that incited quite a frolic among our party, as we stepped on the "Stone of Ecstatic Contemplation," or stood on the "Bridge of the Pillar of the Immortals" and gazed into the "Moon-Washing Fountain." Here the ex-Shōgun with his favorites spent the last years of his life in great luxury, lavishing vast sums on the refined pleasures connected with the cha-no-yu (tea ceremonies).

These ceremonies, peculiar to Japan, which date from the thirteenth century, had first a religious, then a luxurious, and lastly an esthetic stage. The main feature of the religious stage was the Buddhist service, in addition to a simple dinner at which tea was served in place of wine. During the next century the luxurious stage was reached, although it still retained some of its religious character, from the Buddhist pictures of saints and scrolls that adorned the spacious rooms where the entertainments were given. The walls were hung with rich brocades and embroidered silks, gold and silver vessels were used, costly perfumes were burned, and the rarest and most expensive food was consumed. The daimyōs reclined on divans, covered by tiger and leopard skins, while singing and dancing girls entertained the company. Brands of tea were brought in to be tested, and the point of the feast consisted in guessing what plantation produced the materials of each cup of tea. The guest who conjectured rightly was rewarded by a gift of one of the many beautiful ornaments of

Kyoto.

the room. Tea-drinking became a high art, vast sums were squandered, and it gained such popularity among the higher classes and was carried to such an extent that renowned warriors neglected their swords for the teapot or died cup in hand while their castles were being surrendered to the enemy. Schools of tea-drinking were formed, and rules made that prescribed the size of the room and its decorations, the tea service, and all the minor details. Time and change have reduced it to a simple esthetic service, and in this stage we took part in the ceremony in a small room of four and one-half mats in the old palace. The ornaments of the tea-room were a kakemona, an incense burner, and a vase of flowers in the alcove. The beverage is made of powdered leaves, is greenish in color, thick like pea-soup, fragrant, and not very palatable. We much preferred the ordinary infusion. It was served on gold lacquer trays in ancient kaga cups without handles. The etiquette of tea-drinking is peculiar. Seated on our heels in a circle, with a priest to conduct the ceremony, we watched his actions and followed his example, holding the cup with both hands as we consumed the contents. I should like a representation of that scene. The tea ceremony is refined in every detail, but complicated in its forms, and repeated trials grow to be a bore and a nuisance. The general use of tea is a great blessing to the country, as it largely supplants the intoxicating sake, although I strongly suspect they refrain from the latter not from principle but from poverty.

There is a school in the city where the geishas are taught playing, singing, dancing, writing, and embroidery. They are

In Bamboo Lands.

a class by themselves and are apprenticed to their employer at an early age, frequently as young as seven years. They are supposed to have greater personal attractions than girls less favored by nature, but I saw very few handsome ones—for in Japan as elsewhere beauty is not universal—and they were disfigured with powder and rouge, exceeding even their countrywomen themselves.

A GEISHA.

The school occupies a building that encloses a courtyard planted with shrubs and chrysanthemums. We were first shown into a room where a dancing-lesson was in progress. The teacher, a retired geisha, was seated on the floor playing a samisen with a strip of ivory; and in front, on a raised platform, her pupil, with a trace of coquetry, postured, grimaced, rolled her eyes, and twirled her fan in exact imitation of the elder; neither of them appeared in the least disturbed by the presence of half a score of foreigners. We were taken into room after room, where we saw young girls receiving instruction in different branches of education. The choicest bit was reserved until the last; we were ushered into a hall where a number of pupils, each with a samisen, were singing and play-

Kyoto.

ing, and the unearthly discords produced by their enthusiastic efforts were excruciating. It was a competition between time and tune of twelve kinds, not much to the credit of Japanese musical taste. The race is not physically incapacitated for singing—it merely lacks knowledge of music as an art. Having no sweet song-birds, they imitate the shrill screech of the hawk or kite and the melancholy cries of sea-fowl with admirable success. The offer of a performance by finished pupils was gratefully declined; the nervous system could endure no more, and we sought the street to relieve our distracted senses.

A long avenue of grain-fields on one side and pleasure resorts on the other leads to the temple of Nanzenji. While walking up this thoroughfare one afternoon, intent on our guide-book, we were overtaken and accosted by a party of Japanese students in European attire. One of the lads pointed to the open page, and we handed him the book. He read a few words with difficulty, but when questioned talked lamely and was unable to understand us. Obviously they considered it all a huge joke, and lingered near us, laughing and gesticulating, until we reached the temple, where they left us—to our immense relief. They belonged to the new generation, and we were shocked at their brusqueness of manner. They had discarded their national politeness with their national dress. The Japanese have had one undeviating standard set before them for generations, from the Mikado down to the lowest coolie, until they excel all nations in the art of politeness. Until this importation of explosive civilization of the West stirred them up, one century was made the pattern for the next. For ages

In Bamboo Lands.

Japan has worn a dress borrowed from China, and now she casts that aside for the stiff European. During the last ten years, the taste of the people for foreign furniture, furbelows, and food has greatly increased the cost of living. Native domestic economy is reduced to a minimum, and a young couple can begin housekeeping with a few cotton quilts, two kneeling-cushions or mats, a wooden rice-bucket and ladle, a wash-bowl, a few towels, an iron kettle, a charcoal-burner, a tray or two, a teapot, two lacquered rice-bowls, a few china cups, and a bamboo switch for sweeping—all costing about seven dollars.

Happily rid of these hilarious young fellows, we entered the temple, at one time the residence of an ex-Mikado and since converted into a monastery. The main temple, built by Ieyasu, has a floor of dark blue tiles and a rich altar of red and black lacquer adorned with handsome gold images. The walls and pillars are of plain wood, in striking contrast to the richness of decoration. The large two-storied gateway is highly ornate, and the upper room contains two black-lacquered shrines, in which are preserved images of Ieyasu and Takatora its builder. An aqueduct, that serves to convey the waters of Lake Biwa to Kyōtō, crosses the grounds. Its red-brick arches make a pleasing contrast with the greens of trees and shrubs, and add greatly to the picturesqueness of the place.

Paper is one of the chief products of Japan; the mulberry tree not only affords food for the silkworm, but produces a fibre from which the article is made that is remarkable for toughness and elasticity. Over fifty kinds of paper are manufactured; the consumption is enormous, and the uses to which

Kyoto.

it is put are infinite. It is used for windows instead of glass, for fans, handkerchiefs, lanterns, cordage, and many ornamental articles, while oiled paper replaces India rubber and oilcloth for carriage-covering, rain-coats, umbrellas, and tobacco-pouches. One street in Kyōtō is entirely devoted to shops in which paper alone is sold. Writing-paper is put up in rolls; we purchased a packet of envelopes for one sen and writing-paper in ten feet rolls for five sen; but it proved unsatisfactory for correspondence, as the fibre is very porous and the ink spread all over the page. Its being absorbent does not signify with the Japanese, who write with a paint-brush and India ink, and tear off the written portion when the yard or more of letter is finished.

In velvet and silk weaving the Japanese still cling to the old-fashioned hand-looms operated by two persons. Upon entering a factory the visitor is greeted with the incessant crash, crash as the wooden parts come together. We went into one where twenty-five looms operated by foot-power were working at high speed. We also saw the process of boiling and dyeing in a great variety of colors. The cleansed silk was dipped into hot dye, and wrung out by placing a bamboo stick through the skein and twisting it tightly. The dooryard was rendered conspicuous with long pieces of silk of every shade stretched between bamboo poles to dry in the sun. More than one visit was made to these factories of hand-loom weavers, particularly those in which the beautiful velvets are manufactured. Fine brass wires are woven under the nap, and the pattern is painted on before the wires are drawn out for uncut velvet, or

In Bamboo Lands.

cut out for cut velvet. The process requires infinite labor and patience. In every case the head man received us with great politeness, and after leading us through the building he in-

A HAND-LOOM.

vited us into the faultless little garden at the rear, where tea and sweets were served. To relieve the pressure of obligation, we invariably purchased some of his beautiful productions.

Tea, silk, and rice are the three great products of Japan.

Kyoto.

There are frequently serious failures in the latter crop, and the Government is forced to purchase largely from other countries, selling it to the people at cost. The success of the rice-crop being so important, Inari,—the goddess of rice, in the form of a fox—is a very popular deity, as is Daikoku, the smiling god of wealth, who is represented seated on bales of rice. After the rice-planting is over, two days and the intervening night are devoted to merry-making in the temples dedicated to Inari throughout the kingdom. On the outskirts of Kyōtō stands one of the most famous temples of the rice-god. Various superstitions are connected with it, and one legend forms the motive of a Nō drama.

We had arranged to visit Inari on a certain day in the month when pilgrims make the "Circuit of the Mountain Hollows," and, arrived there, we found the temple and grounds thronged with worshippers. A great red Shintō torii stands before the entrance, and at the summit of the steps, on either side, is a stone fox on a pedestal, before which pious mortals had placed offerings of rice to propitiate the gods. Flights of steps lead up to the great courtyard with its rows of lanterns, moss-grown with age. Shintō mirrors, eighteen inches in diameter, hang from the eaves of the main chapel. Not a sign of Buddhism was to be seen, and it was a relief to find, occasionally, a shrine of the old religion unmixed with the imported creed. A priest opened the storehouse to show us the sacred cars, of great age and rich in decorations of gold, silver, and bronze. In these cars the deities of Inari make an annual pilgrimage to Ise, the Japanese Mecca, to which as far as

In Bamboo Lands.

tradition reaches back an extraordinary sanctity is attached. A visit to these shrines is a duty as important to every Shintōist as is the sacred journey to the Mohammedan.

I have one of the little charms carried by pilgrims. It is neatly put up in a paper packet; on a vari-colored background are two grains of rice, on each of which is carved in microscopic proportions a perfect figure of Daikoku, the god of wealth.

Rows of innumerable small red torii mark the beginning of the "Circuit;" numbers of pilgrims were intent on making it, and, not to be outdone by the faithful, we joined the procession. The shrines and inscriptions *en route* lacked interest without explanation, but scenery is not thus handicapped, and admirers of nature can enjoy it in all lands, though each have a different language. On the summit we had magnificent views in every direction of mountains, rivers, villages, and nearer hills fringed with firs, and bamboo fine as feathers. One never wearies of such scenes. The mountain produces the finest mushrooms in Japan, and we saw numbers of our old acquaintances, the trespass notices—but they had lost their power to startle us. Although the circuit occupied three hours, we found our famished kurumayas patiently waiting for us, and to compensate stopped at an inn and supplied them with a full meal well flavored with daikon.

We went to a very good theatre in Kyōtō. A famous play was to be performed, in which the great Buddha himself was represented by the principal character. We rode down the lantern-lighted streets to the entrance, adorned with blood-

INARI.

Kyoto.

curdling pictures in all the colors of the rainbow and rows of gaudy paper lanterns, in front of which was a crowd of theatre-goers and of curious people. Our box in the balcony was furnished with small wooden stools, but otherwise it was abso-

A THEATRE.

lutely bare. When we arrived, the play was in full progress and on the stage were a number of men bound hand and foot, and our guide told us that Buddha would come to release them. He appeared in the form of a white paper horse, drawn along on a cord stretched under the roof from the rear to the front of the building. As he alighted near the prisoners, an actor rushed from the wings and cut the bonds. Then began such

In Bamboo Lands.

an uproar among the players, accompanied by the wildest discords from the musicians, as I have seen but once before—and that was in Sitka, when a party of Indians in war-paint and feathers, with whoops and yells and derisive laughter, each holding a huge rattle in each hand, performed an old-time war-dance for our edification. This revelation of Buddha's power was received by the audience quietly, but with every symptom of approval; for the Japanese never shout, nor applaud with their hands. Another essential accompaniment of our play-houses is lacking—the theatre hat, but it is offset by the custom of allowing an individual to stand up by the payment of a small fee. A practice that obtains on the stage is even more ludicrous: attendants with candles fastened on long poles illuminate the faces of the actors while speaking.

After the excitement had subsided, the feasting, that had been interrupted for a time by the grand climax, was resumed with redoubled resolution. The fact that impresses one most is the continual munching of favorite dainties, such as eggs, rice-cakes, and fruit. It is not etiquette to go to a theatre without previously ordering at a tea-house a lunch to be served during the play. Our cicerone was busy in disposing of the refreshments he never failed to order at our expense, and his appetite was quite equal to the demands made upon it. The building was poorly ventilated; smoking was allowed, as it is in temples and everywhere else. The play had lasted all day, and when we departed at ten o'clock was still unfinished.

The Sabbath has no meaning in Japan—all days are alike;

Kyoto.

business goes on with unresting energy, and unless one is especially careful the day is liable to be overlooked.

By invitation of a clergyman we attended an Anglican service, held in the house of a native convert. The partitions had all been removed, making the house one large room, and the family sat on the stairway during the sermon and looked down upon us. There were about twenty natives present, half of whom had been baptized and the remainder were prepared to receive the sacrament. The service was conducted with dignity and decorum, but being in Japanese was unintelligible to me. The wretched little organ had been imported from England thirty years previous; I was invited to play the accompaniment and consented reluctantly, realizing the ordeal which I was to undergo. A chorus of a dozen voices sang the hymns, which were written in Japanese and set to good old English tunes; but the language is so constructed that it requires a multiplicity of words to express an idea, and it was hard to tell just where the singers were and when they would strike the next bar. However, the last measure we usually finished in unison. There was something very affecting to me in the humble efforts of this little mission, which has been raided more than once—so far without serious results. A party of natives came in during the hour, who, though they took no part in the service, created no disturbance. The clergyman told us that missionaries had great obstacles to overcome in the fickleness of character and extreme indifference of the Japanese to all religion; added to which are the difficulties of the language, making it doubtful for a long period as to

In Bamboo Lands.

whether the words used convey the right meaning or not. And, to crown all, the Japanese students who return from a course of study in Europe proclaim that "they don't believe Christianity in those countries." The whole work of the foreign missionary societies has been little more than a "vast expenditure of energy, time, and money to no real purpose," and I am satisfied that traditionary beliefs, the little "god-shelf" in every home, and the claims of race overmaster all outside influences. No Oriental race has ever yet been converted to Christianity, but God bless whoever tugs at the attempt!

To return to Buddhism—the same afternoon we went to Chion-in to see the unique ringing of the great bell, whose deep tones cause all the buildings in the vicinity to vibrate.

It was a short railway ride to Ōsaka, the commercial centre of Japan. The city has an air of prosperity and comfort; it is intersected by canals flanked on either side by trees; it has countless bridges of stone and timber, and is almost as dependent on its waterways as The Hague. The fortress-crowned and walled castle rises on an eminence whose precipitous sides terminate in the city itself. It was constructed by Hideyoshi in the sixteenth century. The streets are lined with theatres, bazaars, and shops, and the canals are crowded with junks, sampans, and pleasure-boats. The temple of Tennōji is the most celebrated, and the upper story of the pagoda commands a wonderful view of the city and its suburbs. We also went through the Imperial Mint, organized in 1871. In charge of our guide, we spent the evening wander-

Kyoto.

ing through the busy streets, and were impressed by nothing so much as the life on the canals and the islands with their tea-houses and pleasure-grounds. The custom of closing places of business at night does not obtain in Japan, and it

THE OLD CASTLE AND MOAT AT ŌSAKA.

is to be hoped for the benefit of the fortunate visitor that it never will.

The next day we started for Nara, the centre of Japanese Buddhism. It was the ancient capital of seven Mikados from A.D. 709 to 784, and but little of its former splendor remains

In Bamboo Lands.

except the temples and gigantic figure of Buddha. The general aspect of the country is an undulating valley, abundantly wooded and enclosed by mountain ranges brilliantly green with pine-trees. We put up at a semi-foreign inn with a garden bright with autumn flowers and shaded by trees whose branches met above us, drooping under their burden of wistaria. The sun shone warm in that fragrant area, and half the pleasure we received in Nara was from rambling around that enchanting spot, the guide having to summon us twice before we were willing to leave it. Not far from the hotel is a street of shops where local products are displayed, consisting mostly of toy images made of wood and trifles carved from the horns of tame deer, that herd in great numbers in the sacred groves. We passed through rows of stone lanterns that legend states "no man can number"—but women did!—to the handsome dark-red temples shaded by tall cryptomerias. Another avenue with more lanterns, and we reached a building where we were charged an exorbitant price to witness the sacred dance similar to the one seen at Nikkō, but the performers, being young and good-looking instead of grizzled and toothless, were more pleasing to look upon. Among the sights which most attracted us was a fine Buddhist temple that stands on a slight elevation. Great numbers of small bronze lanterns adorn the front, and, seen from this vantage ground, the view up and down the valley and across the town is one of inexpressible beauty. Near by hangs the large bronze bell of Tōdaiji, which, when rung at stated periods, gives out mournfully sweet tones that resound through the

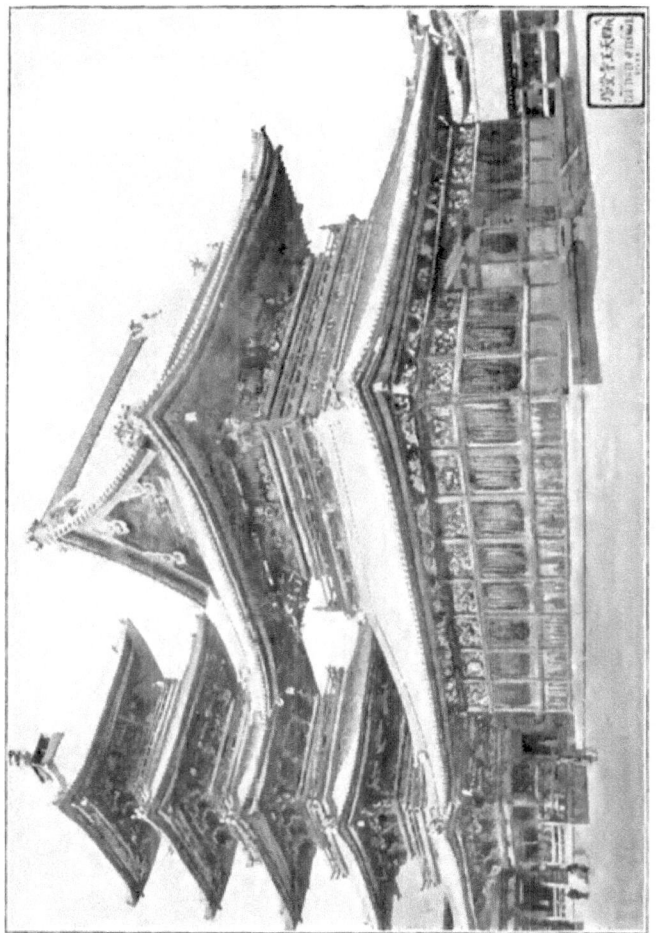

TENNŌJI, ŌSAKA.

Kyoto.

valley. It was cast in A.D. 732 and weighs thirty-seven tons.

The Great Buddha is an immense image, larger than that at Kamakura, but of less merit as a work of art. At first glance its height, fifty-three feet, and corresponding proportions were overpowering. Buddha, with an expression of unsmiling placidity, sat cross-legged on his lotus-leaved throne with a great halo around his head, composed of images of Buddhist deities. The entire figure is made of solid bronze plates. On the altar was the usual array of vases, candle-sticks, incense-burners, and idols. Behind His Majesty we saw an exhibition of venerable hoards of odds and ends. On stands were spread out temple deities, household idols in beautiful lacquer, head-dresses worn on state occasions, pottery and porcelain, musical instruments, ancient swords and embroideries—battered wrecks of time. In the temple of Kōbukuji is carefully guarded the armor of Japan's most popular hero, the great Yoshitsune, born in 1159. A younger half-brother of the Shōgun Yoritomo, he was early distinguished for his valor, but, falling under the displeasure and jealousy of the Shōgun, he fled into Yezo, where he committed harakiri after having previously killed his wife and children. He remains to this day an object of worship among the Ainos, and his name is a synonym with the Japanese for "single-minded bravery and devotion."

The greatest ornament of Nara is the park, where, far removed from the turmoil of the world and the ugly and jarring sights and sounds of our grinding civilization, one seems to

In Bamboo Lands.

breathe an air of purity. In the cool, refreshing shade the inn had provided a delicious noonday meal. The coolies scornfully refused to share the "foreign food," and we gave the surplus to the sacred deer of less fastidious taste. As daylight waned we took the train for Kyōtō, where after hours of sunshine we arrived amid torrents of rain and gusts of wind. The night being chilly, the kurumayas drew us over the ground at a great pace, and we were soon in our rooms enjoying an open fire thoughtfully provided by the presiding genius of that well-regulated hostelry.

The Japanese encourage learning. "During the Middle Ages, education was in the hands of the Buddhist priesthood. The temples were the schools; the subject most insisted on was the Buddhist Sûtras. The accession of the Tokugawa family to the Shōgunate (A.D. 1603–1867) brought with it a change. The educated classes became Confucianists. Accordingly, the Confucian classics, the 'Four Books' and the 'Five Canons,' were installed in the place of honor, learnt by heart, expounded as carefully as in China itself. Besides the Chinese classics, instruction was given in the native history and literature. Some few art students picked their way through Dutch books that had been begged, borrowed, or stolen from the Hollanders at Nagasaki, or bought for their weight in gold for the sake of the priceless treasures of medical and other scientific knowledge known to be concealed in them. But such devotees of European learning were forced to maintain the greatest secrecy, and were hampered by almost incredible difficulties. For the government of the day frowned

Kyoto.

on all things foreign, and more than one zealous student expiated by his death the crime of striving to increase knowledge. With the revolution of 1868, the old system of education crumbled away."

Japan, as "heir of all the ages in the foremost files of time," has selected and adopted the best products of the Occidental brain, and shaped "her acquisitions to meet her own ends." Her military system is modelled on the French and German; her naval system on the French and English; English and American experts constructed her telegraph and telephone systems; and her public school system is modelled upon the best results obtained in Europe and America. In 1872, it was announced officially that "it is intended that henceforth education shall be so diffused that there shall not be a village with an ignorant family, nor a family with an ignorant member." The Japanese are very fond of reading, bookstores are common, and circulating-libraries, carried on the shoulders of men from house to house, are noticed everywhere. We visited the Imperial University and Peeresses' School in Tōkyō; an elementary school for both sexes in Kyōto, where each boy and girl had his or her own seat and desk; and the university called the "Doshisha," founded under the auspices of the Congregational Board of Missions, which occupies with its buildings and grounds a large tract of land in the vicinity of the Emperor's palace. Its success is mainly due to the efforts of the Rev. Joseph Neeshima, an eminent convert and one of the most famous Japanese of modern times. Including the School for Girls, there are more than five hundred students. A lady

In Bamboo Lands.

connected with the female department took us through the buildings, which contain, besides the usual lecture, study, and recitation rooms, a well-stocked library, a fine laboratory, a geological museum, a school of engineering, an astronomical observatory, other minor departments, and the latest scientific apparatus.

One of the corps of instructors remarked: "We hope to do better work when we become better organized."

The boarding-school for girls occupies a building in the same grounds, and is presided over by a principal and several assistants. The girls receive a very good general education, some instruction in music, and are taught to sew—all of which qualifies them to become wives of well-to-do foreigners; but grand failures if they marry natives of their own class, as few Japanese can afford to give their families the luxuries Europeans consider necessities. We were shown about the building and saw the girls at study in their private rooms, after which we dined with the ladies. The ornaments of the dining-room were embroidered scrolls, lacquer-ware, and bronzes; the table appointments were exquisitely refined and the food delicious. The society was the most agreeable of all, and while we conversed there floated toward us the indescribably sweet tones of bells from a neighboring temple. After months of travel and its attendant discomforts it was an hour of enjoyment; we were charmed with everybody and everything. One of the ladies had a fine collection of curios, especially of antique candlesticks, that she had gathered during a residence of some years in the country. The veranda and windows were

Kyoto.

thickly grown with vines and in the garden—although so late in the year—there were still plenty of flowers. I noticed particularly the roses, geraniums, and chrysanthemums. The same evening we went with our friends to a prayer-meeting, held in the house of a missionary. The large parlor was well filled with ladies and gentlemen engaged in ecclesiastical work, and the service of prayer and song was conducted with zeal. The American missionaries are conscientious "teetotallers," and devote their time to their work with praiseworthy energy.

The transition from a solemn Christian gathering to gay street scenes is in Kyōtō absurdly simple. We walked across the park to a native house, where we found the family gathered around the hibachi, as the evening was cool; stepped into our kurumas, and were soon dashing along the street at a speed that rivalled that of a trotting-horse. The route chosen took us through a noted thoroughfare, best seen at night when crowded with people, and lighted its entire length with paper lanterns of every color. Dismissing the kurumayas, who could go no farther, we left them with instructions to await us at a certain point. The theatres, peep-shows, and shops were well patronized. All along the way there were scores of shops filled with the products of patient toil, from articles of dress and ornament to sweetmeats and toys. I bought a box of confectionery containing a dozen varieties invitingly arranged, only one of which I could pronounce good. We saw other places, in which all the articles that could be strung together were hung across the front or in the room, forming great festoons that fluttered with every puff of wind. These ornamen-

In Bamboo Lands.

tal business-signs were especially noticeable in shops where toys and lanterns were for sale. The refreshment booths were crowded, tea and sake, receiving more than their share of attention. We were prepared to see strange scenes and did; and were very careful not to taste anything. Among the thousand quaint sights the people themselves, with childlike satisfaction depicted on their countenances, were always most amusing. All ages were represented, from the patriarch down to the mite napping comfortably or wondering over its mother's shoulder; children are never put to bed until the parents retire. We sauntered up and down, stopping at every little shop, sometimes hemmed in so closely escape was difficult. The whole town appeared to be having a frolic of the first order. The hour was late when, thinking that perhaps we should never meet again, in sad and affectionate words we thanked our charming friends, who had shown us more than kindness, and rode through the waning moonlight to our hotel.

Kyōtō had been an inexhaustible source of pleasure; we had come to see and had not neglected our opportunities. The weeks flew so quickly each day brought new wonders and new pleasures; the Emperor's birthday was at hand, and I had planned to reach Tōkyō on that day, and thither it was necessary to go. Sayōnara.

CHAPTER VII.

MUTSUHITO AND HARUKO.

A NIGHT ride in a Japanese sleeping-car, without accommodations for sleeping other than the leather-cushioned seats, is a novel experience and affords a rare opportunity to study the people. Rather than be the only occupant of a carriage reserved for ladies, I took a seat in one well filled with natives, I being the only foreigner. The passengers all belonged to the Samurai class, their narrow, pale faces, arched noses, thin lips, large eyes, white teeth, and a certain hauteur of manner indicating the indelible caste distinction. I bundled myself up in a corner and napped between stations, although disturbed somewhat by the ceaseless chatter they kept up during the entire night, and the tap, tap of smokers removing the ashes from their pipes.

A SAMURAI.

The Japanese are the soul of refinement, as evidenced by much I saw during my tour; and never was it more apparent

In Bamboo Lands.

than during that night's ride. An elderly gentleman and his son had seats near me, and while having our respective breakfasts we exchanged courtesies, I offering fruit and eggs—of which all classes are very fond, he giving, in return, rice-cakes that nearly choked me while attempting to swallow them. I shall never forget an incident that occurred at daybreak. Suddenly I noticed every passenger with head uncovered, gazing in a reverential manner out of the windows; I too looked—and saw Fujiyama as I had never before seen it. What a glorious sight it was! Reddening in the sunrise, with not a cloud to obscure it, the great dome of snow stood forth in all its majesty, bathed to its summit in rosy tints. We were running through the lowlands at the base of the mountain, and the view was peerless. On my first visit to the Pacific Coast I waited many days for the clouds to pass that obscured Mount Hood, and when at last the great snow mountain appeared in the extreme excitement of the view its beauty and grandeur quite unnerved me. A similar emotion influenced me on that lovely autumn morning when Fujiyama revealed itself covered with snow and glistening in the slow splendor of the increasing sun. A grand climax to all I had seen in Japan and a rich compensation for a restless night in a stuffy car. It is not surprising that the Japanese worship with profound reverence this noble mountain, for these snow-crowned peaks cannot fail to rouse the noblest emotions in mankind.

After this grand sight—which I have longed ever since for a painter's power to place on canvas—we reached Yokohama.

Mutsuhito and Haruko.

A *déjeuner à la fourchette* concluded, I started with friends for a garden on the Bluff to see a fine exhibit of chrysanthemums (kiku), then in their prime. Magnificent plants of every conceivable color bordered the paths, and in temporary arbors, put up to protect them from the sun, were masses of them.

A VIEW OF CASTLE, AND NIJIJBASHI.

Some plants were allowed to bear but one blossom, and single specimens of enormous size, fastened on twigs, were stuck in the ground in patterns, making a pleasing variety. This flower-display can be duplicated in no other country but Japan. The day was so charming we continued our ride to Mississippi Bay and lunched at our favorite tea-house. The same evening found us nicely housed at the Imperial Hotel in Tōkyō.

In Bamboo Lands.

At last came the much-desired November 3d, the Emperor's birthday—happily it was fine—and we prepared to attend the festivities in his honor. The vast enclosure of the imperial palace, once the castle of the Shōguns, stands in the centre of the city, protected by eleven miles of moats and high stone walls, the blocks of which are fitted together without mortar or cement. Three broad moats filled with aquatic plants in autumn and wild fowl in winter, and ramparts one hundred feet high in some places, surround the grounds. Turret-shaped towers surmount the angles, and there are twenty-seven entrance gates, some of them approached by bridges, the finest of which is the Nijiubashi, a beautiful structure of white marble. The gardens which surround the palace are extensive, and every detail is carried out in accordance with the best schools of Japanese landscape-gardening. Mountains, lakes, streams, fountains, bridges more or less imposing in size, rocks, dwarfed pines, and shrubs are ingeniously arranged to form a natural scene. The grounds are beautifully cared for and thickly planted with forest trees that antedate the memory of the oldest inhabitant by a century or more. Magnificent chrysanthemums—the royal flower of Japan—in bloom, transformed the spot into a garden worthy of Amyitis.

Few Japanese and no foreigners are allowed to enter the grounds, unless their presence is there desired.

The ancient palace was destroyed by fire in 1872 and the work of rebuilding begun in 1884. Architecturally the modern one is in pure Japanese style. The cluster of low white build-

Mutsubito and Haruko.

ings, with black-tiled roofs, covers an area of fifty-six hundred square yards. Walking up the broad avenue and "entering through long corridors isolated by massive iron doors, we find ourselves in the smaller of two reception-rooms, and at the commencement of what seems an endless vista of crystal

THE PALACE.

chambers. This effect is due to the fact that the shoji, or sliding doors, are of plate glass. The workmanship and decoration of these chambers are truly exquisite. It need scarcely be said that the woods employed are of the choicest description, and that the carpenters and joiners have done their part with such skill as only Japanese artisans seem to possess.

In Bamboo Lands.

Every ceiling is a work of art, being divided by lacquer ribs of a deep brown color into numerous panels, each of which contains a beautifully executed decorative design, painted, embroidered, or embossed. The walls are covered in most cases with rich but chaste brocades, except in the corridors, where a thick embossed paper of charming tint and pattern shows what skill has been developed in this class of manufacture at the Imperial Printing Bureau. Amid this luxury of well-assorted but warm tints remain the massive square posts, beautiful enough in themselves, but scarcely harmonizing with their environment, and introducing an incongruous element into the building. The true type of what may be called imperial esthetic decoration was essentially marked by refined simplicity —white wooden joinery, with pale neutral tints and mellow gilding. The splendor of the richly painted ceilings, lacquered lattice-work, and brocaded walls was reserved for Buddhist temples and mausolea. Thus we have the Shintō or true imperial style presenting itself in the severely colorless pillars, while the resources of religious architecture have been drawn upon for the rest of the decoration. In one part of the building the severest canons have been strictly followed; the six imperial studios, three below-stairs and three above, are precisely such chaste and pure apartments as a scholar would choose for the abode of learning. By way of an example in the other direction, we may take the banqueting hall, a room of magnificent size (five hundred and forty square yards) and noble proportions, its immense expanse of ceiling glowing with gold and colors and its broad walls hung with the cost-

Mutsuhito and Haruko.

liest silks. The throne chamber is scarcely less striking, though of smaller dimensions and more subdued decoration. Every detail of the work shows infinite painstaking and is redolent of artistic instinct. The furniture of the palace was imported from Germany."

Twenty-five years ago the person of the Emperor was so sacred he was seen by no one save high court officials, and even to them his face must be veiled. When he first appeared in public he was clad in the national costume. He now visits the charity hospitals and drives about the streets as the rulers in Western lands. The Emperor and Empress received their guests surrounded by princes of the imperial blood and officers in full dress, with the long coat confined by a silver belt, such as German soldiers wear, and stiff little caps with a great white aigrette, like the French. The Emperor Mutsuhito is slightly above the average Japanese height, and though not handsome has an air of distinction. His eyes are dark, his short hair as black as ebony, and his beard is trimmed à la Française. He wore the full-dress uniform of a general in the army. He is a man of great force of character, of much energy and endurance, and devoted to outdoor sports—riding, shooting, tennis, fishing, and football. This wise and unselfish ruler was born in 1852. The Empress Haruko was *en grande toilette* of Parisian make. She is petite, has jet-black hair, a finely formed head, much personal beauty, and is a very clever woman. She is two years older than her husband. She has organized many charities, benevolent societies, and a school for the daughters of noblemen, where they receive instruction in English

In Bamboo Lands.

branches, music, drawing, and painting. The lace-schools are under her patronage, and she interests herself also in silk-culture and embroidery. The Empress is both a poetess and a musician; her favorite instrument is the koto of seventeen strings, on which she is an accomplished performer. The

THE EMPEROR.

Crown Prince Haru, born in 1879, is being carefully educated, and already speaks English, French, and German fluently. Two little princesses complete the group. All are deeply imbued with Western ideas.

The sentiment of the Japanese toward the royal family is not only one of religious veneration for the representatives of an unbroken dynasty which dates back twenty-five centuries, but also one of affection for each individual member of it. The government is a limited monarchy. A tidal wave of foreign ideas reached Japan in 1886, and since that time the Japanese court has abolished the national costume, although it is said that the Empress still wears the native dress in private. They endeavor to be everything that is Western and nothing that is Eastern.

A FLOWER-VENDER.

Mutsuhito and Haruko.

We thought it a piece of barbarism to discard the easy, graceful kimona for the stiff, ill-fitting European costume; for, with all our superior civilization, we cannot teach them anything about dress, and why, with all the world to choose from, they should choose ours is inscrutable. Before leaving the country I was gratified to learn that a reaction had set in; the highest intellect of the country strongly resists this servile imitation of the West, and it is to be hoped that, if Japan resumes her national dress, she will never again abandon it. I deplore the denationalization of nations, the breaking up, in short, of national life and customs; and instances of it are numerous—India rapidly becoming Anglicized; Hawaii a Republic; Japan imitating Europe. The times threaten to deprive these countries of their peculiar charm. The change is most remarkable in Japan, where the worship of ancestors and the ancient customs form the national religion.

THE EMPRESS.

It is quite the rule for the Mikado to abdicate in favor of his successor; he then rises to the rank of ex-Mikado. This

In Bamboo Lands.

custom extends to all classes; a father upon reaching middle age gives up business in favor of his son, and waiting for "dead men's shoes" is not a fashionable occupation. After seeing something of the Orient, one feels quite inclined to doubt whether our ideas of civilization are the highest and best, after all.

We saw the review of local troops by the Emperor, who was on horseback and made an impression by his fine and soldierly bearing. He was attended by mounted men, with plumes waving, and their bugles blowing the notes of their own march. It was a festal day. The city was decorated with thousands of flags; the Japanese ensign, a red ball on a white ground, and His Imperial Majesty's portrait was everywhere displayed. Bands of music played the national air and modern war-tunes; through the streets flowed a great multitude in gala attire; and each hour a train arrived from which a crowd poured forth. As night came on the excitement increased, and there was a marvellous illumination extending as far as the eye could reach; the whole city was ablaze with lanterns, and fireworks, the favorite national combustible, were discharged in large quantities.

It was the good fortune of the writer to meet a typical family of the highest world. The husband was dressed as a European, the wife wore the native costume, although she was educated in America. Their house was of Western architecture, and in the admirable grounds, shaded by grand old trees, bloomed a wealth of shrubs. The interior was fitted up with great elegance; and, seated on damask-covered chairs, we

A SHINTŌ SHRINE, KŌBE.

Mutsuhito and Haruko.

had tea with our hostess, a lady of many accomplishments, Oriental ease of manner, and richly attired in an embroidered kimona. She conducted us through the house to the upper rooms, which contrasted strongly with those below. Fine white mats covered the floors, kakemonos of great beauty were suspended from the toko walls, and vases of freshly gathered flowers brightened the pretty interiors. Nowhere in the world are such delicate attentions lavished upon the visitor as in Japan. Family life among the upper classes, a life of which foreigners see little, is sacred, and to speak to an Asiatic of his wife and daughters would be a gross rudeness and an unpardonable insult. A foreigner, though admitted to the house of a Samurai, sees nothing of the domestic life, and his reception in the guest-room is usually most formal. Our Japanese friends sent parting gifts, accompanied by the usual shred of seaweed neatly put up in a gilt-paper packet. The bit of seaweed signifies the origin of the race and good luck, and the custom of sending it with presents is universal.

At Aoyama, the residence of the Empress-Dowager, and Dangozaka we saw the most wonderful displays of chrysanthemums in the world.

CHAPTER VIII.

THE INLAND SEA.

Sir Harry Parkes' two daughters, a commodore of the English navy, the manager of the steamship company with his wife, and three Americans composed the party who sailed on the *Empress of India*. As we stepped on board the ship that was to bear us away, baskets of flowers were presented by the gentleman who has made the Grand Hotel the finest hostelry in the East.

The scenery was sublime as we dropped down the bay. The volcano on Vries Island sends heavenward an eternal cloud of smoke, and snow-crowned Fujiyama towers over the hills into the deep blue sky, forming a picture neither poet nor painter can depict. Continually coming into view are outlying islands richly clothed with vegetation that comes down close to the water's edge, rocky promontories, and inlets thickly studded with little white-sailed boats engaged in fishing. A blue sky, a smooth sea, the weird cries of seabirds enrich a scene that makes the blood dance in the veins. As the sun travels westward and sinks below the horizon, its last rays light the cliffs and the sea with a golden glow.

We remained on deck long after

THE INLAND SEA.

The Inland Sea.

> "the moon,
> Rising in clouded majesty, at length
> Apparent queen, unveiled her peerless light,
> And o'er the dark her silver mantle threw."

The following morning we cast anchor in the land-locked harbor of Kōbe, the seaport of Ōsaka. It was crowded with shipping—men-of-war, English and other foreign tramps, Japanese mail-boats, junks, and sampans, mixed up with coal-barges and steam launches. Kōbe in bad weather is probably as dismal as most places, but on that bright November day it wore a decidedly picturesque appearance. The hills, tinted with autumn's many-colored leaves, offered great attractions for those who could walk well, and, as we all could, the instant breakfast was finished we started for the heights.

In going to the famous cascades formed by a mountain stream that leaps a hundred feet into the pool below, we were constantly beset by beggars, who made special effort to display their repulsive deformities. It was a pretty stiff climb of two hours, past torii, temples, and tea-houses and sound of chanting brooks, to the summit where stands the shrine dedicated to Maya Bunin, the mother of Buddha. Ranges of mountains somewhat bare rose to the west, and over the bay, between us and Izumi, the shores for miles are exquisitely beautiful; the woods run into the water. Coming down, we heard a peculiar rustle among the trees; and discovered a troop of wild monkeys indulging in a lively frolic. The walk had given us sufficient exercise, and we were glad to engage kurumas for the remaining sights. A fine driveway runs along the sea-wall,

In Bamboo Lands.

and higher up is another avenue, where we saw a gorgeous show of chrysanthemums, equal in quality if not in quantity to other flower displays. Continuing our ride, we crossed the unruly Minato-gawa by a massive stone bridge to the native town of Hiogo; visited several noted temples and a wonderfully fine statue of Buddha fifty feet in height; rummaged among the curio-shops; and returned late that evening to our steamer.

There were no late sleepers the next morning; every passenger was on deck when the ship weighed anchor, for we were about to thread the waters of the beautiful Inland Sea—a long strait that stretches for two hundred and forty miles between the main islands from Kōbe to Shimonoseki. It is thickly studded with islets—some large, thickly populated, and under a high state of cultivation; and others mere nameless rocks, a foe to seamen. Mountains rise to a height of seven thousand feet, villages abound on the shore, temples and ruined castles can be distinguished among the trees, and square-sailed junks and fishing-craft ply the smooth water. From time to time we passed among islands so closely grouped they appeared to form a *cul de sac;* but the skilful pilot steers the ship in safety round point after point, encountering currents and whirlpools that have sent many a native boat to destruction. The course is well lighted, and can be traversed equally well by day or night. The lovely island of Miyajima is one of the "three chief sights of Japan," a resort of pilgrims, and so sacred that no one is allowed to be born or to die there. Its famous temple is built on piles, over the water, the great torii stands in the sea, and the sacred deer are as tame as those at

MIYAJIMA, THE GREAT TORII.

The Inland Sea.

Nara. The climate is delightful; and fine tea-houses and good bathing combine to make it a popular watering-place.

The peculiar beauty of the famous sea is derived from the bold and diverse outline of the islands, the little rocks, and the varied vegetation; its praises have been sung for ages, and its wonderful loveliness has been at once the inspiration and the despair of painters and of poets. The scenery is much more picturesque than that of the Thousand Islands of the St. Lawrence River, and less grand than that of the Inland Passage to Alaska.

We reached Nagasaki early in the day. As we entered the harbor the celebrated island of Pappenburg was seen rising Gibraltar-like from the sea. In the seventeenth century thirty thousand native converts were thrown over its high cliffs by command of Iemitsu, who drove out the Jesuits and extinguished Christianity.

The Christian religion has had a hard struggle in Japan. Beginning with the arrival of St. Francis Xavier in 1549, the new theology early in the next century had gained about six hundred thousand converts. The government became alarmed at its spread and, fearing its influence, determined to suppress it. The Christians defied the ruling power, and rebellion, sieges, and massacres followed, ending with the wholesale slaughter of Pappenburg. The converts met their fate with courage, refusing to trample on the cross. The new faith was completely obliterated. Griffis explains the larger success of the Jesuit missions of the sixteenth century partly by the resemblance between the outer forms of Roman Catholicism and

In Bamboo Lands.

the outer forms of Buddhism—the newer being taken for a higher form of the older, though, "in point of dogma, a whole world of thought separates them from every form of Christianity." Hecker classes it as one of the "epidemics of the Middle Ages."

At that time the Dutch were the principal traders in Japan, and after an agreement not to proselyte had been duly executed a colony of them was allowed to occupy the "walled and bridge-guarded" island of Deshima, a suburb of Nagasaki, for trading purposes. There is a humorous side to the corralling of these traders, for, as is well known, the Hollanders of that period had little interest in saving souls—their sole ambition was to save silver. They would have been much more dangerous neighbors if either greater sinners or greater saints. This agreement so readily made was as easily kept, and for two hundred years, until the arrival of Commodore Perry in 1853, the Dutch monopolized the trade of the country.

The sheltered harbor, a narrow inlet three miles in length, is one of the most famous in the world, and affords safe retreat for all classes of shipping. It is also an important coaling-station. We had no sooner cast anchor than great flat-bottomed boats were moored alongside, and a tireless crowd of native girls and boys passed the coal in small baskets up the gangway and discharged it on board. It would seem to be a slow process, but the little army worked uncomplainingly all day, and by evening we had the necessary supply of fuel.

The sun lighted up the island as we stepped on board the

NAGASAKI.

The Inland Sea.

sampan of the English Consul, that landed us at the European settlement. Pretty bungalows, embowered in greenery—the homes of foreign merchants—cling to the steep hillside; and on a conspicuous point the Stars and Stripes wave above the consulate. A short distance up the bay is the point where the American astronomers observed the transit of Venus in 1874. At the wharf were guides and kurumayas galore, clamoring for business, and, having but one day for sightseeing, we lost no time in securing both.

We rode along the water-front past consulates, public buildings, banks, business houses, and clubs to the native town, where we spent a few hours in the fascinating curio-shops. Silks, embroidery, tortoise-shell and fine porcelain to tempt the most indifferent were lavishly displayed. I purchased a miniature karuma made of tortoise-shell that lasted two hours, and some beautiful designs in pottery that lasted longer. We also visited a bazaar that occupies the old prison-house of the Hollanders. By steep streets and stony lanes we reached the Shintō temple of Ō'Suwa, of no great interest aside from the huge bronze horse that adorns the courtyard and the extended view over the town and harbor from the garden. An atoshi was hired for each little carriage, and we hastened on to Moji, five miles distant by an excellent road, celebrated for its fine scenery; the hills on both sides, terraced to the summit, are planted with tea and rice. Moji is a wretched little village, charmingly situated on the seashore. From a point beyond we had a grand view of Shinabara Gulf, and lunched at a tea-house whose balcony overlooked the water.

In Bamboo Lands.

Had we not been running a race with time, a walk back to town would have been more to our taste than the prosaic kuruma.

We first made short visits to a Buddhist temple and a res-

A BUDDHIST TEMPLE.

taurant of note; then we climbed the hills where oaks, camphor-trees, and bamboo shaded the paths, and wild flowers grew in profusion. The summits are covered with moss-grown gravestones.

During the annual "Feast of the Dead" or "Festival of Lanterns," fires are lighted at night on the hill-slopes and the

ON THE ROAD TO MOJI.

The Inland Sea.

cemeteries are brilliantly illuminated with lanterns and thronged with relatives of the departed. Special devotions are performed, and offerings of food are placed before the family graves for the benefit of deceased friends who are supposed to return to earth for a short period. Nagasaki is noted for its religious festivals, which are still observed with all the gorgeous display and enthusiasm of ancient times. The Suwa Festival, the most magnificent of all, is held in October. As I did not see it, I will quote from Fischer, who did: "First goes an immense shapeless mass of linen carried on a bamboo by a stalwart man, of whom nothing can be seen but his feet. Mighty is the load he bears, for the cloth is full twelve ells in length and embroidered throughout, forming one huge canopy. Then come banners and embroidered ornaments, covered with skilful needlework, representing some renowned man or celebrated woman, a hill covered with snow, the instruments of various trades, or scenes from ancient Japanese history. Next follow musicians, playing upon drums, cymbols, and flutes, strangely attired and accompanied by a number of servants. These are led or headed by the ottona, the chief municipal officer. Then appears a long train of children, representing some expedition of one of their mikados or demigods. This part of the show is most admirable; clad and armed like the warriors of former times, the leaders march gravely along, followed by the representatives of an imperial court, male and female, displaying the greatest pomp and luxury and surpassing every conception of dainty beauty. Each of these trains is attended by a number of palanquins,

In Bamboo Lands.

which are intended for any of the children who may become fatigued. After these come companies of actors; every now and then high benches of equal size are ranged along the road, and on these the actors perform with great spirit and emphatic gesticulations. Their actions are accompanied by the music of flutes and syamsen (shamisen). When this is over, a crowd of miscellaneous musicians, palanquins, servants, and the relatives of the children follow, and this closes one train."

WRESTLERS.

Madame Chrysanthème and the cottage where she resided with her French husband were not *en évidence;* but Pierre Loti's charming sketch made the whole environment seem strangely familiar. It was just twilight when we arrived on board with the crushed tortoise-shell—however, we did not mind that much! At last the moment of departure arrived, and we bade farewell to Japan—that land of many charms, fairy world of inexhaustible interest, Eden of the nineteenth century. On leaving the country, I realized that a few months spent there had enabled me but to stumble over the threshold; to understand her institutions, to see things from their point of view, and to know the unique workings of the

The Inland Sea.

Asiatic brain would require a long residence and continuous study for years. One will best see the Orient by looking through the eyes of the Oriental.

We sailed away, and two days later were in China.

GLOSSARY OF JAPANESE WORDS.

Amado, outside shutters used at night.
Arigato, "Thank you."
Asarum, a plant whose leaf is the crest of the Tokugawa family.
Atoshi, a man who pushes the kuruma from behind.

Buddhism, a religion introduced from China via Korea in the sixth century.

Cha-no-yu, the tea ceremonies.
Compradore, an agent or middleman.

Daibutsu, Great Buddha.
Daikon, a radish.
Daimyō, a feudal lord.
Dai Nippon, Great Japan.
Dashi, a car used in religious festivals.

Fusuma, sliding screens covered with wall-paper.
Futon, a bed-quilt.

Geisha, a professional player, singer, and dancer.
Geta, wooden clogs.
Godown, a fire-proof storehouse.
Gohei, an emblem of Shintōism used in temples.

Harakiri, suicide performed by thrusting a sword into the abdomen.
Hata, a flag.
Heimin, the common people, of whom there are 35,000,000.
Hibachi, a charcoal brazier.

Ichō, the name of a tree whose leaves turn gold in autumn.
Ihai, funeral tablet bearing the "dead name" that a Buddhist receives to be known by in the next world.
Ikura, "How much?"

Glossary of Japanese Words.

Kago, a small palanquin used in travelling and borne on the shoulders of two men.
Kagura, a Shintō dance.
Kakemono, a hanging scroll.
Kami-dama, a Shintō shrine-shelf.
Kamiyo, the "dead name" of a Buddhist.
Kimona, a loose, long-sleeved robe worn by both sexes.
Keyaki, Japanese elm, used in the nave of temples.
Kiku, the chrysanthemum.
Kóchō, the head man of the town.
Koku, about five bushels, a standard measure of capacity.
Ku, a city ward.
Kuruma, a jinrickisha or man-power carriage.
Kurumaya, the kuruma runner.
Kwazoku, the nobles, about four thousand in number.

Maro, a loin-cloth six inches in breadth.
Mate, "Stop!"
Matsuri, a religious festival.
Mon, the crest, or coat-of-arms.
Mousme, a young girl.

Nō, a lyric drama patronized by the nobility.
Norimono, a palanquin used by the nobility.

Obi, a sash worn by women.
Ohyo, "Good morning."

Rin, a copper coin of which a thousand make a yen.
Robiton, a bowl.

Sake, rice beer, containing from eleven to seventeen per cent. of alcohol.
Sampan, a shore boat.
Samurai, a two-sworded man, a retainer of a feudal lord.
Satsu, paper money.
Sayōnara, "Good-by."
Sen, a cent, a hundredth part of a yen.
Shintō, the indigenous religion.
Shintō mirror, an emblem of the Shintō faith.
Shizoku, Samurai, two-sworded men, of whom there are about two million.
Shōgun, a great military general, or Tycoon.

Glossary of Japanese Words.

Shoji, a sliding screen covered with translucent paper, that serves as a window.
Soraban, an instrument enclosing rows of beads sliding on thick wires used for figuring.

Tabako-bon, a tray with fire-pot and ash-pot used by smokers.
Tatami, a house-mat made of rushes, 3 feet by 6 feet and 2½ inches thick.
Tempo, a copper coin worth about eight rin, coined A.D. 1830-1844.
Tokonomo, an alcove.
Tokugawa dynasty, beginning with Ieyasu in 1603 and ending in 1867.
Torii, literally, birds' rest, a portal before the entrance to a Shintō shrine.

Waraji, a straw sandal.

Yadoya, an inn.
Yashiki, a mansion.
Yen, a Japanese dollar.

Zen, a lacquered stand six inches in height, a dining-table for one person.

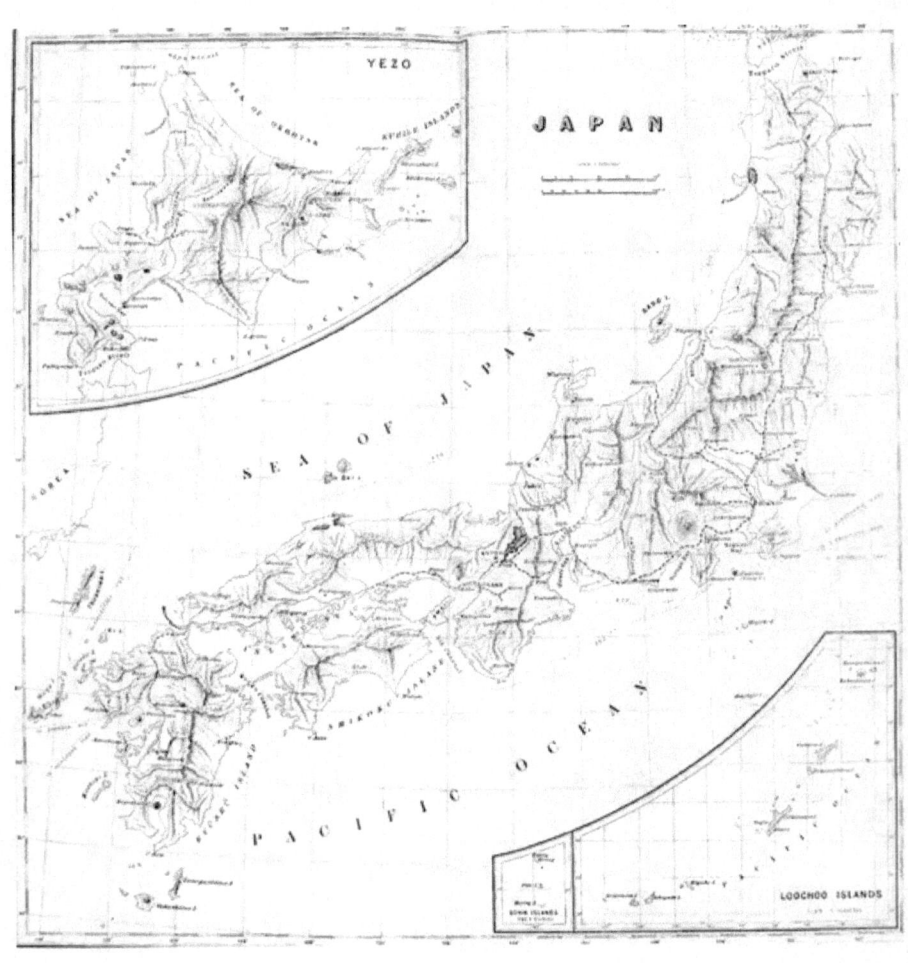

www.ingramcontent.com/pod-product-compliance
Lightning Source LLC
Chambersburg PA
CBHW030345230426
43664CB00007BB/541